Aspects of Applied Geography

MARTIN DUDDIN

URBAN CHANGE AND ITS MANAGEMENT

Jim Bruce, Alan Doherty and Malcolm McDonald

Series editor: Martin Duddin
(Assistant Rector, Knox Academy, Haddington)

Hodder & Stoughton

A MEMBER OF THE HODDER HEADLINE GROUP

ACKNOWLEDGEMENTS

CONTENTS

The author and publishers thank the following for permission to reproduce material in this book:

Blueprint Magazine, Figures 5.1–5.10; Doubleday, Figure 5.11; HMSO, Crown Copyright ©, Figure 2.13; Office of Population, Censuses & Surveys, Figure 2.24, reproduced with the permission of the Controller of Her Majesty's Stationery Office © Crown Copyright. Routledge; Figure 2.22.

The publishers would also like to thank the following for giving permission to reproduce copyright photographs in this book:

J Allan Cash Ltd, Figures 1.10, 2.17; Robert Harding, Figures 1.8, 2.34; Hutchison Library, Figure 2.18; Panos Pictures, Figure 3.13; Sylvia Cordaiy, Figure 2.6; Topham, Figure 2.24.

All other photos including the cover belong to Alan Doherty.

Every effort has been made to contact the holders of copyright material but if any have been inadvertently overlooked, the publishers will be pleased to make the necessary alterations at the first opportunity.

British Library Cataloguing in Publication Data

Bruce, Jim
    Urban change and its management. – (Aspects of applied geography)
    1. Urbanization 2. Cities and towns 3. Sociology, Urban
    I. Title II. Doherty, Allan III. McDonald, Malcolm, 1951–
    307.7′6

ISBN 0 340 62097 8

First published 1996
Impression number   10 9 8 7 6 5 4 3 2
Year   1999 1998 1997

1 **Population and Urbanisation**   page 3
    An Historical Perspective
    Population Explosion
    Urbanisation
    The Growth of Cities
    The Growth of 'Millionaire' Cities
    Developed and Developing Cities

2 **Case Study: London**   page 10
    UK: Population Growth and Urbanisation
    London: Physical Growth and Structure
    London: Socio-Economic Growth and Structure
    Managing Change in London
    The London Docklands

3 **Case Study: Karachi**   page 31
    Pakistan: Population Growth and Urbanisation
    Karachi: Growth and Structure
    Managing Change in Karachi
    Karachi: Squatter Settlements

4 **Urban Growth: Problems and Solutions**   page 43

5 **Assignments**   page 45
    Doughnut London
    Edge Cities

    Bibliography   page 48

    Glossary   inside back cover

307.26   Y2016939

Typeset by Litho Link Ltd, Welshpool, Powys, Wales. Printed in Great Britain for Hodder & Stoughton Educational, a division of Hodder Headline Plc, 338 Euston Road, London NW1 3BH by Redwood Books, Trowbridge, Wiltshire.

Front cover photo
Karachi roundabout: town meets country © Alan Doherty

POPULATION AND URBANISATION

KEY CONCEPTS

LOCATION, CHANGE, SPATIAL PATTERN, DIVERSITY

Throughout the twentieth century more and more people continue to move into towns. So much so, that the biggest migration movement anywhere in the world is that from rural to urban areas. An increasingly large proportion of the world's population is now urban. It is therefore very important for geographers to study towns and cities in order to try and understand the reasons for their growth and development, and to analyse their characteristics and problems.

This text examines the phenomenon of increasing urbanisation and in particular looks at managing the problems facing urban areas. The focus is on a contrast between London, a city in a More Economically Developed Country (MEDC) and Karachi, one in a Less Economically Developed Country (LEDC).

An Historical Perspective

The process of urbanisation (an increasing proportion of the world's population living in towns) probably evolved during the Neolithic Period (New Stone Age) around 5000 years ago. In the fertile river basins of the Middle and Far East, the domestication of seeds and animals, and the use of the wheel, ox-drawn ploughs and irrigation meant that some groups of people were able to produce an agricultural surplus. This allowed them to settle in one place, with nomadism giving way to the growth of small settlements. When this happened some people were freed from food production and could specialise in things like woodworking, pottery and metal-forging, with the trading of these goods also possible.

The earliest towns were probably in the Tigris and Euphrates Valleys in what was then known as Mesopotamia, and these were soon followed by towns in the valleys of the Rivers Indus, Nile and Yangtze (see figure 1.1).

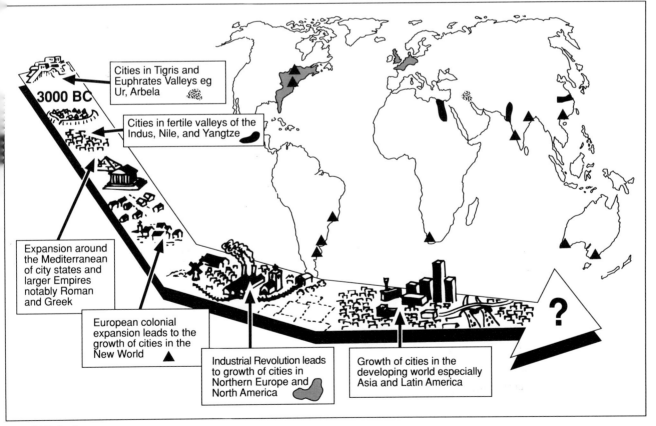

Figure 1.1 Early urban centres

3

By the tenth century BC, many city states had grown up around the Mediterranean Sea, and this in turn led to the growth of the Greek civilisation, and the Roman Empire.

The Romans were responsible for the founding of hundreds of towns across Europe, and many have grown to become great cities of modern times, such as London, Paris, Cologne, Lyons and Bordeaux.

The fall of the Roman Empire by 395 AD led to a decline in the development of towns throughout Europe, the Middle East and North Africa. The tribes responsible for the overrun of the Empire were either farmers or herders, and had little need themselves for large towns geared to a quite different lifestyle from their own. Only in the later Middle Ages (1300–1450 AD) did towns such as Paris and London become hubs of trade and commerce which encouraged further urban growth.

In the eighteenth and nineteenth centuries, the improvements in agriculture, developments of manufacturing and continued trade with the colonies led to a rapid growth of towns and cities across many parts of Europe, Asia and North America. During this period of European colonial expansion, settlements such as Boston, Rio de Janeiro and Sydney were established and grew as centres of commerce and administration in the New World.

Population Explosion

As can be seen in figure 1.2, it was not until the early years of the nineteenth century that the estimated total population of the world reached 1000 million. Yet by the early part of the twenty-first century, only 200 years later, it is predicted to reach 6–7000 million people.

This huge growth came about because of long-term changes in the birth and death rates. The death rates fell throughout the world because of:

- *improved food production and diet;*
- *better housing conditions;*
- *improved sanitation.*
- *greater availability of drugs and medicines;*
- *vaccinations and preventative medicine;*

In the LEDCs the process lagged behind and was often related more to the eradication of endemic and epidemic diseases than to the limited success of housing, sanitation or health improvements in many countries. Birth rates have not fallen as much in LEDCs and the increased difference between the birth and death rates has led to a rapid population growth with many associated social and economic problems. This is especially true in South East Asia (see figure 1.3).

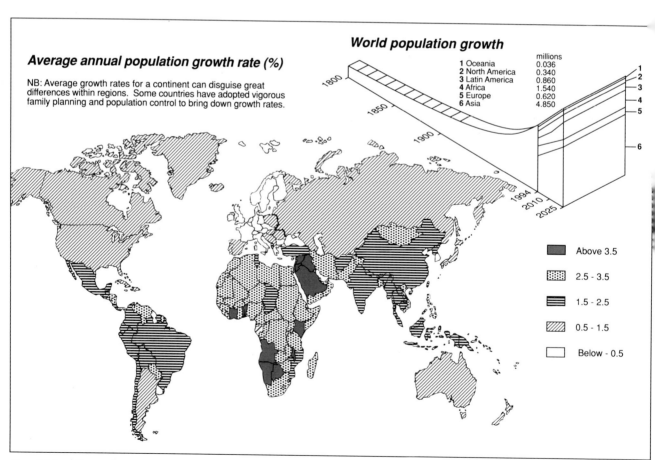

Figure 1.2 Population growth

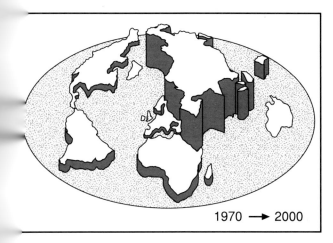

1970 → 2000

ure 1.3 Population growth rates

Urbanisation

As the world's population has grown, the proportion of people living in towns and cities has also increased. This process, known as urbanisation, has occurred in two overlapping phases.

In the nineteenth century in Europe and North America, as a result of the Industrial Revolution, many people were attracted to the towns and cities to find employment.

- *In many LEDCs, in the period since the 1939–45 war, there has been a massive move to the cities, partly in search of work, but often simply as an escape from the poverty and deprivation of rural life. It may also be the case that the natural growth rates in these cities will be higher because of the proportions of young immigrants who are of child-bearing age.*

Urban areas throughout the world face huge problems, such as providing adequate housing and water supplies. However, the scale of the problem is much greater in the large cities of LEDCs, swollen as they are with huge numbers of migrants from the surrounding rural areas. The rapidly increasing percentage of urban populations can be seen in figure 1.4.

At the turn of the century only about 10 per cent of the world's population lived in urban areas, but the average figure was approaching 60 per cent by the mid-1990s. In Europe the figure is closer to 75 per cent urban, while in South East Asia the degree of urbanisation is still far below that, at about 30 per cent. By the 1990s, the urban system of living (or aspiring to it!) had become the established way of life in almost every part of the world.

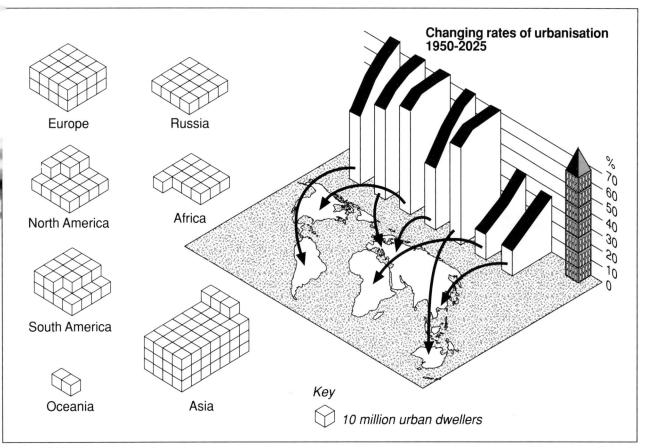

Figure 1.4 World urbanisation

5

Figure 1.4 on page 5 shows the increasing rates of urbanisation in the different continents and the number of people living in different areas.

1 **World population is increasing geometrically rather than arithmetically. What does this mean?**

2 **Which continents have a rapidly rising population?**

3 **In the nineteenth century Europe's rate of population growth was often as great as it is now in the LEDCs. What was the 'safety valve' which enabled the European countries to cope with the increase in numbers?**

4 **Which areas have shown the greatest rises in levels of urbanisation?**

5 **Describe the ways in which the growth of large cities might be seen as (a) an advantage and (b) a disadvantage to the economic growth of LEDCs.**

6 **Using figure 1.2 name four countries with high population growth rates (more than 3.5 per cent per annum).**

7 **Name six countries with growth rates less than 0.4 per cent.**

8 **Can you identify any pattern in the distribution of countries with very low growth rates?**

The Growth of Cities

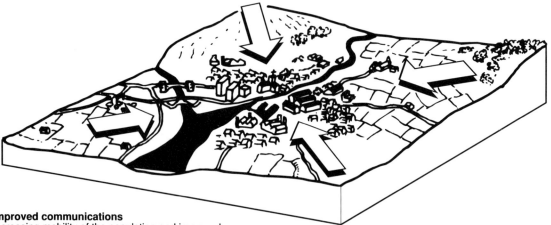

Industrial development
The development of industries leads to the growth of towns and cities. This happens when factories benefit from being clustered together near sources of power, raw materials, water supplies, services or labour. Therefore houses, shops and offices tend to concentrate in certain areas as the key industries expand, thus attracting more people and further growth.

Changes in farming
In Europe the Industrial Revolution led to farming practices being more efficient and a reduction in the amount of farm labour. This led to rural depopulation on a large scale throughout the nineteenth and twentieth centuries. In many LEDCs rural depopulation is more often related to the severe difficulties people face, such as drought, soil erosion, regular flooding, crop pests and diseases, civil unrest and war.

Improved communications
Increasing mobility of the population and improved knowledge of the opportunities in towns and cities via mass media lead to a greater influx of people into the cities. Transport improvements include the expansion of the rail networks in the nineteenth century, both in MEDCs and LEDCs, and the advent of road transport in the twentieth century.

Urban services
Within towns and cities the availability of basic services like health and education is better than in rural areas. This often disguises great disparities between the richer and poorer areas of a large city.

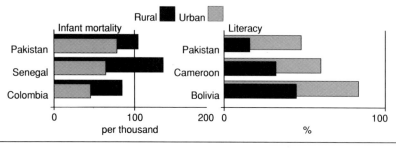

Health and education are a lot easier for governments and local authorities to provide in cities. Mortality rate and literacy rates for many developing countries show up the advantages of living in the cities.

Figure 1.5 The growth of cities

6

IMATE CITIES

[...]ile the process of urbanisation in MEDCs led to [...]wth in many towns and cities, in LEDCs this [...]wth is often concentrated in a very few cities. [...]is has sometimes led to the situation where the [...]gest city can be many times larger than the [...]ond largest city. This **primate city** is usually the [...]ital, and it tends to dominate the economy of the [...]ntry. It attracts more immigrants than other [...]rts of the country, preventing growth taking place [...]ewhere, and creating futher problems within the [...]y itself. Sometimes two closely related cities can [...]mbine to create this same effect, for example if [...]e is the main port for the capital city.

This phenomenon is more marked in Africa and [...]tin America than anywhere else. The examples [...]hich follow are therefore all taken from these two [...]ntinents and figure 1.6 shows the population of [...]e primate city (or group of cities), the population [...]the next largest city, and the total population of [...]e country concerned.

	Population			
	Primate city (millions)	Second city (millions)	Country	Population (millions)
Santiago	4.0	0.5	Chile	12
Mexico City	11.5	2.0	Mexico	85
Lima	3.5	0.5	Peru	20
Quito	2.0	0.2	Ecuador	10
Lagos	5.8	1.2	Nigeria	110
Accra	1.2	0.2	Ghana	14
Nairobi	1.1	0.6	Kenya	21
Cairo	8.5	0.4	Egypt	47
Kinshasa	2.5	0.7	Zaire	33

Figure 1.6 Primate cities

The Growth of 'Millionaire Cities'

Not only is there a larger proportion of people living in cities, but there has been a corresponding rise in the largest of these cities. Cities of over 1 million people are often known as **millionaire cities**. In 1800, London was the only millionaire city in the world. By the beginning of the twentieth century, there were still only 11 millionaire cities across the world, but since then there has been a rapid rise and there are now nearly 200 in all.

The distribution of the millionaire cities has remained fairly constant throughout this century, with approximately 30 per cent in Europe, 40 per cent in Asia, 20 per cent in North America, and 10 per cent in South America. Africa and Australasia have very few millionaire cities.

A notable feature of the growth pattern of these cities is the fact that while the earlier ones appeared in the higher latitudes, more recent ones have been appearing ever closer to the Equator. For example, in 1920 there were about 25 millionaire cities, and their average latitude was 45°. By 1990 the number of millionaire cities had grown to nearly 200, with an average latitude of 33°. It is in some of the LEDCs that the growth of these cities is at its fastest. This can be seen as a reflection of the rapid growth of the population of these areas, as well as the increasing urbanisation.

WHY ARE THEY SO LARGE?

Many millionaire cities have grown because they are, or have been, the political capital of the country concerned. This can add further status to a city which is already attractive to incomers because of other factors, and explains, for example, why Rio de Janeiro is so large, even though it is no longer the capital of Brazil. Similarly Karachi (see Chapter 3) continues to expand, although the capital of Pakistan is now Islamabad. In both these cases the new capital was set up to counter the primate city syndrome and provide a new growth point closer to the geographical centre of the country.

Many capital cities have so dominated the economic life of the country concerned that they have also become primate cities. Paris is a good example of this, so much so that a major part of the French Government's economic policy in recent years is to actively encourage development in the provinces. These policies are designed to break the dominance Paris exerts over the economy, and to allow industrial growth to occur in other parts of France.

HOW MUCH BIGGER WILL THEY GET?

Many of the cities which have attained 'millionaire' status have in fact far exceeded that level, and have become '5 million', or even '10 million' cities. There were only two '5 million' cities in 1920 (New York and Buenos Aires), yet by 1980 this number had risen to 17 (including Tokyo, Peking, Mexico City and Rio de Janeiro).

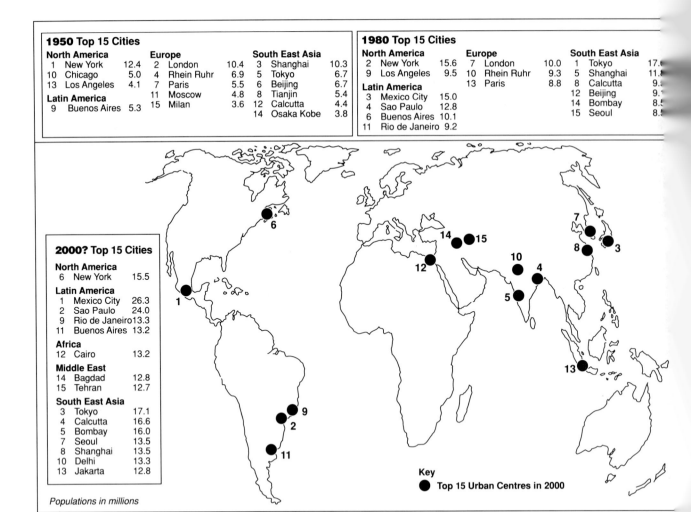

1950 Top 15 Cities					
North America		**Europe**		**South East Asia**	
1 New York	12.4	2 London	10.4	3 Shanghai	10.3
10 Chicago	5.0	4 Rhein Ruhr	6.9	5 Tokyo	6.7
13 Los Angeles	4.1	7 Paris	5.5	6 Beijing	6.7
Latin America		11 Moscow	4.8	8 Tianjin	5.4
9 Buenos Aires	5.3	15 Milan	3.6	12 Calcutta	4.4
				14 Osaka Kobe	3.8

1980 Top 15 Cities					
North America		**Europe**		**South East Asia**	
2 New York	15.6	7 London	10.0	1 Tokyo	17.?
9 Los Angeles	9.5	10 Rhein Ruhr	9.3	5 Shanghai	11.?
Latin America		13 Paris	8.8	8 Calcutta	9.?
3 Mexico City	15.0			12 Beijing	9.?
4 Sao Paulo	12.8			14 Bombay	8.?
6 Buenos Aires	10.1			15 Seoul	8.?
11 Rio de Janeiro	9.2				

2000? Top 15 Cities	
North America	
6 New York	15.5
Latin America	
1 Mexico City	26.3
2 Sao Paulo	24.0
9 Rio de Janeiro	13.3
11 Buenos Aires	13.2
Africa	
12 Cairo	13.2
Middle East	
14 Bagdad	12.8
15 Tehran	12.7
South East Asia	
3 Tokyo	17.1
4 Calcutta	16.6
5 Bombay	16.0
7 Seoul	13.5
8 Shanghai	13.5
10 Delhi	13.3
13 Jakarta	12.8

Populations in millions

Key

● Top 15 Urban Centres in 2000

Figure 1.7 Largest urban centres

Similarly the number of '10 million' cities has grown in the 1970s and 1980s, and there are now approximately ten cities of this size across the world, and many more are rapidly approaching that number.

The growth of some of these cities has begun to slow down, however, as the process of **counter-urbanisation** takes effect, especially in MEDCs. In many cases the slowing down of the growth rate is actively encouraged by both local and national governments but may be caused by pollution, congestion, and the cost of living.

Developed and Developing Cities

When geographers are looking at cities in MEDCs and LEDCs it is perhaps too easy to stereotype their characteristics. Cities have always been dynamic entities, bringing with them specific problems linked to growth, landscapes and the management of change. However, there are some similarities which can be identified, that support the idea that towns and cities do have common features no matter in which part of the developed or developing world they are located.

Figures 1.8–1.12 introduce some of the general issues involved in the management of these different urban environments before Chapters 2 and 3 study two typical examples in more detail.

9 **Identify aspects of running cities which figures 1.8 to 1.12 and the front cover suggest will need managing or planning in some way. You may use the same answer for more than one photo. Make a list for each photo.**

10 **Using housing as an example, make two lists (one for cities in MEDCs and the other for cities in LEDCs). In each case, state the main problems which will confront city planners or managers.**

11 **Repeat Question 10 for the issue of transport. Use figures 1.8 and 1.11 to help you.**

Figure 1.8 London: managing transport in the ageing developed city

Figure 1.9 Karachi: housing contrasts
a) An old squatter settlement
b) Farm engulfed by urban sprawl

Figure 1.10 London: coping with suburban sprawl

Figure 1.11 Karachi: traffic problems

Figure 1.12 Karachi: provision of utilities
a) Watering of sports ground in middle-class school
b) Tanker supplying water to recent squatter settlements

SUMMARY

- THE RAPID RISE OF THE WORLD'S POPULATION IN THE LAST 100 YEARS HAS SEEN A GREATER PROPORTION OF PEOPLE LIVING IN LARGER SETTLEMENTS.
- MORE AND MORE OF THE LARGEST CITIES IN THE WORLD ARE FOUND IN LEDCs.
- THIS GROWTH HAS LED TO TREMENDOUS PROBLEMS OF URBAN MANAGEMENT WHICH ARE SIMILAR IN BOTH MEDCs AND LEDCs.

2 CASE STUDY: LONDON

UK: Population Growth and Urbanisation

In the United Kingdom today 80 per cent of the population can be classified as urban. With an already high population density (57 million people living on a group of islands of 244 034 km^2), this has implications for the country in terms of 'urban sprawl'. This is the apparently incessant growth of towns at the expense of rural land areas. It is estimated that by the year 2010, almost 30 per cent of the land area of the UK will be built upon.

This growth of urbanisation in the UK is relatively recent in historic times, as is the overall population growth. Even by the time of the Doomsday survey in 1086, there were less than 2 million inhabitants in the UK. Growth throughout the medieval period meant that by 1700 the population had only risen to around 6 million. Figure 2.1 shows the rapid changes which followed during the Industrial Revolution and into the twentieth century. By 1851 the urban population had grown to around 50 per cent and by 1901 it had risen to 75 per cent.

It can be seen, therefore, that in a relatively short time the UK changed from a rural society, dependent on agriculture, to an urbanised society, dependent on industry and commerce.

Three main stages of urban growth can be distinguished in the UK.

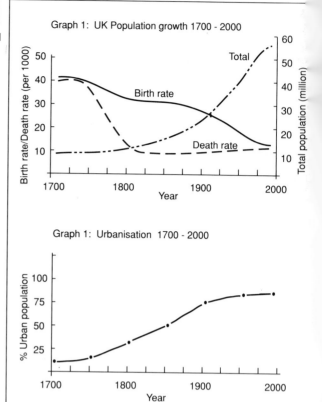

Figure 2.1 UK population growth and urbanisation, 1700–2000

1 The Roman occupation

Most of Britain in the first century AD was under Roman occupation, and only the area north of Hadrian's Wall remained free of permanent Roman rule. The population south of the wall at that time was around 500 000 and much of that was concentrated in the south east. London was the largest urban concentration, with around 15–20 000 people. Other towns (*coloniae*) such as York, Lincoln, and Gloucester had on average 3–4000 inhabitants. Many modern cities can trace their history right back to this period of Roman occupation. This reflects the fact that the sites were very well chosen by the Romans (e.g. route centres, bridging points, resorts etc).

Medieval growth

When the Romans left Britain, urban growth [sta]gnated for some time. The Norman conquest [br]ought increased political stability and the [ex]pansion of medieval settlement began. This [pe]riod is characterised by the development of a [la]rge number of market towns, separated from each [ot]her by a relatively short distance. These towns

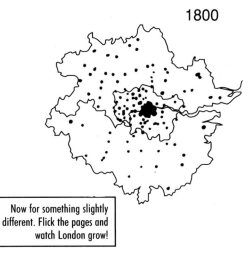

Now for something slightly different. Flick the pages and watch London grow!

served their surrounding area, providing a meeting place and market for the barter and sale of agricultural produce. Early settlements were small, and often enclosed for security, but as trade expanded and settlements in favoured locations grew, they took on a recognisably urban character.

3 Industrial Revolution

By the eighteenth century many smaller villages and towns began to expand rapidly, since they were located close to raw material sources needed for the industries of the period. Most of these new towns were located, therefore, on or near the major coalfields of Britain, in the Midlands, North East England, Central Scotland and South Wales. Birmingham, for example, grew from a population of around 2000 in 1650 to 750 000 by 1911. This meant that there was a major redistribution of the population, away from the South and East and into the North and West of the country (see figure 2.3, page 12).

DISTRIBUTION OF UK POPULATION

Figure 2.3 shows the present distribution of the population in the UK. It is obvious that there is great disparity in the densities across the country. In England as a whole the figure is 350 people per

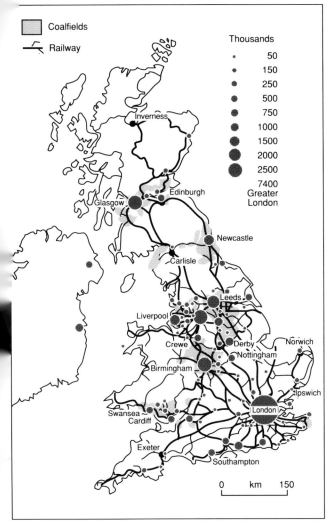

Figure 2.2 Industrial towns, railways and coalfields in the British Isles

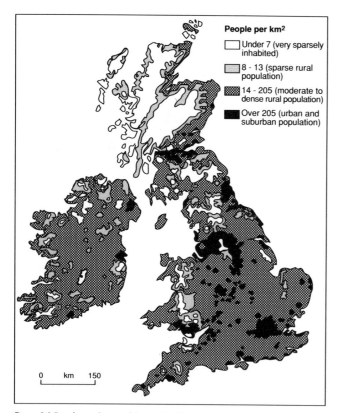

People per km²

- ☐ Under 7 (very sparsely inhabited)
- ▨ 8 - 13 (sparse rural population)
- ▩ 14 - 205 (moderate to dense rural population)
- ■ Over 205 (urban and suburban population)

0   km   150

Figure 2.3 Population density of the British Isles

km² while in Scotland it is only 65 per km². However, even here there is a big variation between the industrialised Central Belt, and the Highlands to the north. In fact, over half of the UK's population lives in the area from Greater London to South Lancashire and West Yorkshire. Although the patterns have changed with the rise and fall of the older heavy industries, London and the South East have continued to be the main focus of industrial growth and population expansion.

TOWNS AND CITIES TODAY

As a result of the changing pattern of urban development over the three stages, towns and cities in the UK can be classified under three headings. Many are still recognisably *market towns*, e.g. Carlisle, Penrith, Lincoln, and the towns of the Scottish Borders like Hawick, Galashiels and Kelso. Most of the larger towns and cities have become *industrial centres* based on the nineteenth century industries near the coalfields, e.g. Birmingham, Leeds, Newcastle, Sheffield, Glasgow, Cardiff. Many of the other large cities with newer industries have grown because of their excellent road and rail accessibility, e.g. Luton, Swindon, Bristol. Some towns have specialised functions which help maintain their importance and give them the status of *administrative centres*. These include ports (e.g. Glasgow, Liverpool,

Bristol, London) or resorts (e.g. Brighton, Blackpool, Bournemouth) or cultural/educational centres (e.g. Oxford, Cambridge). Many cities also have administrative and financial functions and serve as regional or national capitals.

As these towns have expanded, suburban growth has eaten into the surrounding countryside, and the various functions have grouped in recognisable zones within the town. Some of these zones, particularly in the inner cities, are the centres of many of the urban problems encountered today, e.g. slum housing, unemployment, crime and industrial decline.

London is the largest and most complex urban area in the UK. It is larger than the next ten cities in the UK put together in terms of population. London is more than a mere capital city. It is a **primate city**, dominating the economy, government, social development, and cultural evolution of the UK.

In addition, London is also a **world city**. For four centuries London has conducted trade and transactions on a world scale. Around 60 per cent of Britain's largest 500 industrial firms have their headquarters in the City. On an international basis only New York has a higher proportion than London of the world's top 500 manufacturers' headquarters. London obviously remains a major control point despite its relative decline in terms of population. The largest city in the world a century ago, London now ranks twentieth in terms of population. It must be noted however that the cities which have overtaken London (e.g. Los Angeles, Tokyo, Mexico City, Bombay, São Paulo) have not been subjected to 40 years of stringent planning controls, designed to contain London's sprawl within a protected **green belt**. This planning collar inadvertently intensified linkages between the core (Greater London) and an ever increasing hinterland in South East England, creating a 'dispersed metropolis'. We shall now examine this complex, integrated city region.

DEFINING LONDON

London refers to the area that was covered by the Greater London Council until its abolition in 1986, i.e. the 32 boroughs and the City of London (see figure 2.4).

The City of London refers to the square mile at the heart of the capital which exists as a separate independent local government unit.

Inner London refers to the 12 most central London boroughs and the City of London, the area which was administered by the London County Council until 1965. (The same area was administered by the inner London Education Authority (ILEA) from 1965 to 1990.)

12

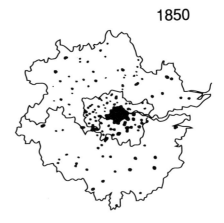

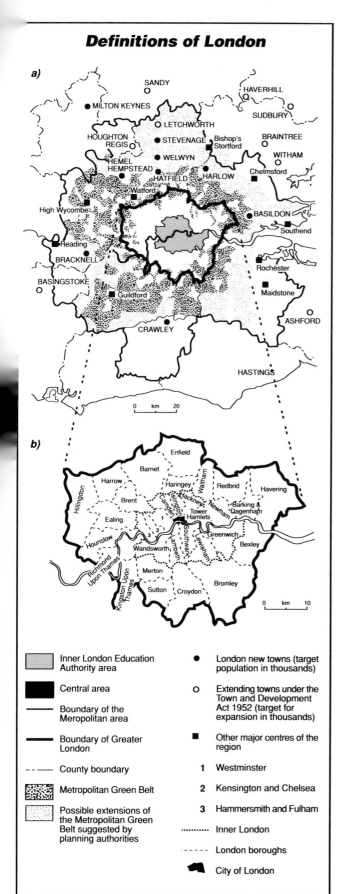

Definitions of London

a)

b)

	Inner London Education Authority area	•	London new towns (target population in thousands)
	Central area	○	Extending towns under the Town and Development Act 1952 (target for expansion in thousands)
	Boundary of the Meropolitan area		
	Boundary of Greater London	■	Other major centres of the region
	County boundary	1	Westminster
	Metropolitan Green Belt	2	Kensington and Chelsea
	Possible extensions of the Metropolitan Green Belt suggested by planning authorities	3	Hammersmith and Fulham
		....	Inner London
		- - - - -	London boroughs
			City of London

Figure 2.4 a) London boroughs b) the London region

Outer London comprises the remaining 20 boroughs that made up the area covered by the Greater London Council.

It can be argued that London cannot now be contained by the limits of the old Greater London Council, or by the M25. The region which London influences stretches out into the Rest of the South East, (RoSE), and even beyond (see figure 2.4).

1 **What were the main reasons for the increasing urbanisation in the UK?**

2 **The Romans left their mark on nearly two-thirds of the British landscape. What evidence, if any, is there of the Roman occupation in your area?**

3 **Name examples of market towns, industrial centres, and administrative centres in your local region.**

4 **Use an atlas to work out the top ten cities in the UK's urban hierarchy.**

5 **Patrick Geddes was the first to coin the concept of a world city. In what way is London a world city? Why is size relatively unimportant when considering the criteria which makes a city a world city?**

London: Physical Growth and Structure

London was established during the Roman invasion of 45 AD. A well located port protecting maritime, military and later domestic supply routes, the City offered an ideal base for further military operations to the north. It is not accidental that London seems to look back to Europe; this indeed was the intention of the conquering colonial power.

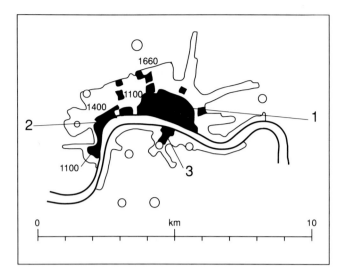

Figure 2.5 The early growth of London with unification of the Cities of London and Westminster along the Strand on the north bank of the River Thames
1 Expansion east and north east of radial route ribbon development, followed by infilling of the back land 2 Development west and north west was partly planned, e.g. Lincoln's Inn and partly unplanned 3 South of the River Thames the original bridgehead settlement grew slowly

Figure 2.6 Present day London skyline

The Romans were also responsible for London's core structure. Their forum was sited virtually where the Bank of England stands today and the remains of their initial square fort can still be seen in the Barbican complex. The Romans protected their City behind a wall, and eventually built a bridge across the then shallower and wider River Thames to the south bank at what is now Southwark. This 3 km wall effectively enclosed London until medieval times when Edward the Confessor instigated a major ecclesiastical and royal building development to the west of the Roman walls at Westminster. This separate City of Westminster became the focus for court and administrative activities. The 'old' City continued to dominate commerce and trade in the South East, while the

south bank of the Thames became the favoured location for playhouses, brothels and manufacturing. For the first 1500 years of its existence, then, London was largely contained by its original Roman walls. Housing densities gradually rose until London, bursting at the seams, finally began to expand (see figure 2.5). This radial expansion occurred along all the major routes out of London and was accompanied by considerable urban renewal in the old core, an activity which was given even greater impetus by the Great Fire of London in 1666, when nearly three-quarters of the City burned to the ground.

The fire presented an unsurpassed opportunity to indulge in urban remodelling on a monumental scale. Plans were drawn by Christopher Wren amongst others, but in the event very little changed. The in-built inertia of a complex property-owning pattern ensured the survival of the original street pattern almost in its entirety. Only two new roads were built, although under new building regulations many streets were widened. The same post-fire building regulations were to limit all non-ecclesiastical buildings to a height of 30 m until well into the twentieth century. The precious nature of this architectural inheritance was not generally acknowledged until it had been lost in the twentieth century skyline of high-rise blocks (see figure 2.6).

Until the nineteenth century, London was a pedestrian city which grew but remained compact and nucleated (see figure 2.7). The gentry had their carriages and there was heavy cart traffic – so heavy that there was a campaign to ban brewers' drays from certain streets in London. Like the campaigns to ban chariots from ancient Rome and motor cars from twentieth-century central London, it was not completely successful! However, the vast majority of Londoners walked to and from their daily business.

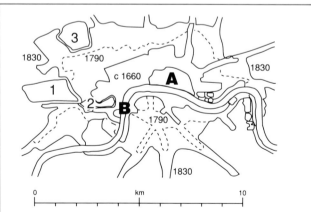

The growth of London showing three stages (1660, 1790 and 1920) related to the City of London (A) and the Whitehall area of the City of Westminster (B). Three royal parks are shown: 1 Hyde Park; 2 Green Park and St James's Park; 3 Regent's Park.
In 1830 the major constraint determining London's physical expansion was the lack of public transport, a factor which was overcome from the early years of the railway age.

Figure 2.7 The growth of London from the sixteenth to nineteenth centuries

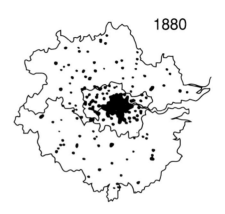

1880

...is pedestrian mode of transport meant that the ...ntre of London was clearly the best place to live. ...e worst slums therefore, were to be found just ...tside the walls of London on the very edge of the ...ty. This state of affairs continued until the advent ...the horse-drawn omnibus in 1829. A decade later ...d another technological advance, the suburban ...ilway, meant that the pace of the flight to the ...burbs quickened and the complete separation of ...ork place and living quarters could take place.

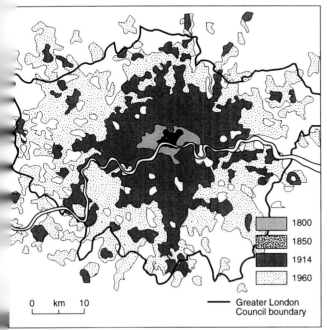

	1800
	1850
	1914
	1960

0   km   10

——— Greater London Council boundary

Figure 2.8 The suburban spread of London during the nineteenth and twentieth centuries

The situation of home and work being invariably in the same building, if not in the same room, had existed in medieval cities. It was during the Renaissance that they were gradually separated and from 1600 onwards eating and cooking were separated from sleeping – at least for the merchant and professional classes. When houses were first divided into separate rooms each room was accessed by passing through other rooms, but by the seventeenth century rooms were reached along corridors like houses along streets. Privacy or living space, therefore, became a more and more sought-after commodity in urban life but remained the preserve of the better off until the adjacent nature of home and work could be broken. Technological improvements in transport severed this cord and enabled the burgeoning City to radiate outwards along ten well-defined transport corridors. London's infamous suburban spread had started (see figure 2.8). Steam trains ran further along the same routes previously used by the horse-drawn vehicles, which in turn would later be replaced by the automobile.

At first sight it may seem surprising that having developed a reasonable transport system and a promising overall plan (even if by luck rather than by sound management), nineteenth century pre-industrialised London should become a post-industrialisation nightmare to be escaped from by everyone who could afford a suburban house and a commuter's season ticket. To understand we must now examine the socio-economic fabric of the city and in particular the effect, and continuing inheritance, of the Industrial Revolution.

London: Socio-Economic Growth and Structure

For centuries London remained a remarkably compact city with a population of around 35 000 in 1377 which grew steadily to around 200 000 by 1600 (see figure 2.9). London's population growth then accelerated rapidly despite the setbacks of the Plague and the Fire, doubling its population in the seventeenth century to 550 000 in 1700, and again during the eighteenth century to just over 1 million at the first census in 1801, and yet again in the first half of the nineteenth century to just below

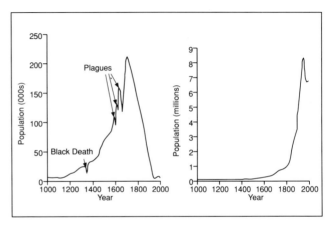

Figure 2.9 London and Greater London: population

2 million. By 1881 the population had reached 4.5 million and by 1911, 6.5 million. Coping with this population explosion and its accompanying urban sprawl remains London's most enduring problem. But as has been noted above, London did not expand much physically until the mid-nineteenth century when the advances made in mass transportation enabled it to spread. In addition, the advent of the Industrial Revolution meant that London's population wanted to move outwards.

The economist, Hammond, described the Industrial Revolution as *'a storm that passed over London and broke elsewhere in cities such as Manchester, Leeds, Birmingham, and Glasgow.'* Granted, London's experience of the Industrial Revolution was unique. However, although London was not noted for mining and heavy engineering, it was certainly not spared the economic and social upheaval associated with the industrialisation of the UK in general.

The importance of the service sector, particularly transport, finance and commerce made London's experience unique (see figure 2.10). Although this importance has been under-estimated in the past, it is now generally recognised that the service sector contributed more to Victorian economic growth than manufacturing. London's economy has been characterised by its dynamism and versatility. This has been due to the following factors.

- *The dominance of the service sector. Tertiary industry has provided a relatively stable employment base as this sector has traditionally been far less susceptible than manufacturing to cyclical fluctuations.*
- *The city's manufacturing base is, nevertheless, broad and diverse. It is not profitable for a region to have the majority of its workers in one industry.*
- *The size and wealth of the London market has ensured that demand for local products remains high.*
- *Urbanisation itself stimulated growth by creating demand for a variety of products, services and amenities such as processed foods, transport and cleaning services, and entertainment and leisure facilities which would not otherwise have been required.*
- *Within the home, the decline of domestic servants from the turn of the twentieth century, coupled with the provision of electricity, provided the basis of the sharp rise in the demand for household appliances such as vacuum cleaners, washing machines and fridges. Domestic consumer goods therefore, have always been a mainstay of London's economy.*

During the nineteenth century it was clothing, shoemaking, furniture, printing, metals, engineering and precision manufacturing which were the most important trades. In the twentieth century, other consumer industries such as electrical engineering and vehicle manufacturing grew in importance whilst the more traditional trades started to decline.

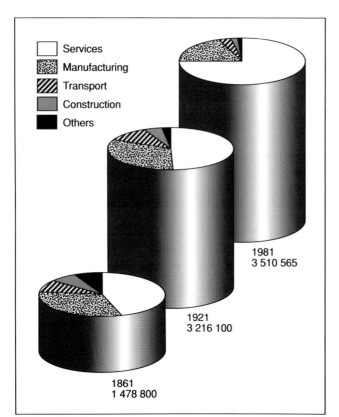

Figure 2.10 Employment in Greater London, 1861–1981

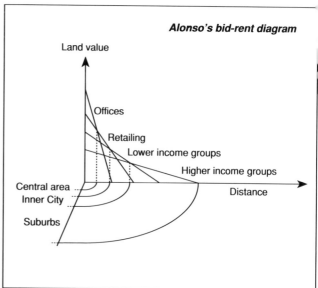

Figure 2.11 Urban land use segregation

Land values rose more quickly in the central areas (near to jobs and markets), than on the edge. Poorer groups were pushed out to the cheaper sites on the edge of the City or into ever denser housing conditions in the East End. This residential segregation within the City, based on the ability to pay for land (see figure 2.11), was soon followed by a dramatic upheaval of population. By 1860 only

mmercial enterprises could afford the high rents
the desirable central sites. Between 1861 and
81 the rateable value of the City of London
bled while its population halved! This exodus was
rtly voluntary and partly forced due to demolitions
r warehouse construction, street clearances and
ilway building. For example 40 000 occupants of
ms were decanted from the City in order to build
rringdon Street. As the residential population
ll, the number of jobs in London rose from
70 000 in 1866 to 301 000 in 1891. Those who
uld afford to use the commuter transport lines
ft for the suburbs, whilst the remainder were
queezed into the already densely settled inner
eighbourhoods.

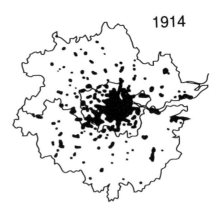

1914

Figure 2.12 The lure of the country

The concern with the conditions in which the
working classes lived which resulted in the
introduction of bye-laws to control the construction
of housing so as to create a safer and more healthy
environment. The latter part of the nineteenth
century also saw an upsurge in civic pride as city
corporations assiduously laid out public parks
(check the date of your local park!), cleared their
slum housing, and constructed roads, water mains
and sewers. The introduction of worker's fares (as a
condition of the railway companies being allowed to
extend their lines through areas of demolished
working-class housing) led to the creation of huge
working-class suburbs, such as Tottenham,
Edmonton and Enfield, or Walthamstow and
Leyton. London now grew and grew.

The London Underground extended its lines out
into the open countryside, planned bus routes to fan
out from the new stations, and waited for
developers to complete the cycle of profitability (see
figure 2.12). There were no planning restrictions to
dampen the fire of **suburbanisation** and a wave of
bricks and mortar and humankind moved outwards
from the old core. Simultaneously, migrants from
the rest of Britain and later from the
Commonwealth moved in to the core to feed the
City's considerable appetite for cheap labour. After
a temporary lull during the 1914–18 war,
suburbanisation picked up again during the 1920s
when a further 810 000 people decanted towards
the periphery. Several reasons for London's growth
are apparent.

- *The Depression cut the costs of both materials and labour in the construction industry.*
- *The agricultural depression meant that 'a farmer's best crop was a crop of bungalows'.*
- *The continuing growth of white collar employment provided a huge market and stable incomes, even in the depths of the Depression.*
- *Interest rates were at a minimum.*
- *The fledgling New Town movement also made a contribution to the movement of population in the 1920s by attracting Londoners even further afield with promises of garden cities and local employment.*
- *Planning controls were also at a minimum. The Town Planning Acts of 1909, 1924, and 1932 were simply not fully exercised.*

So London grew and alarm bells started ringing as
more and more fertile market gardening land
disappeared.

6 In what ways did the Great Fire of London in
1666 prove to be beneficial to London?

7 List the various ways in which mobility was
improved in London in the nineteenth century.
How did these changes affect land use and
population densities in central London?

8 List and comment on the push and pull factors which fuelled the great increase in London's nineteenth-century population.

9 London's manufacturing base is broad and diverse. In what way has this been beneficial to the city's economic development?

10 What is meant by the term industrial agglomeration?

Managing Change in London

By the late 1930s the ever onward march of the speculative builders provoked a strong reaction from academics and administrators. As more and more traditional countryside was seen to be lost, various arguments were proposed to change and control urban sprawl.

- *The loss of so much high quality agricultural land was condemned by geographers such as Dudley Stamp.*
- *The loss of rural heritage was denounced by planners such as Patrick Abercrombie. The influential Council for the Preservation of Rural England was instituted.*
- *Frederick Osborn and others campaigned for the decanting of population into Garden Cities similar to Letchworth or Welwyn.*
- *Others argued for the decentralisation of industry, contrasting the growth of London with the depression of areas such as North East England and the West coast ports, where up to 50 per cent of the workforce remained unemployed. If industry could be persuaded to locate in the depressed northern coalfields, then not only would these regions be helped but also the migration flow and growth of London could be slowed.*
- *There was also a vociferous and particularly influential NIMBY (not in my back yard!) brigade, who bemoaned the taste of the builders and their lower middle-class clients.*

In 1937 a Royal Commission on the Geographical Distribution of the Industrial Population (which is more commonly referred to as the Barlow Report) concluded that: '. . . *the continued drift of the population to London and the Home Counties constitutes a social, economic and strategical problem which demands immediate attention.*'

This judgement, given in 1940, proved to be the most important single influence on the creation of the modern British planning system. The Barlow Report spawned a series of studies and reports, including Patrick Abercrombie's *Greater London Plan* which was published in 1945 (see figure 2.13).

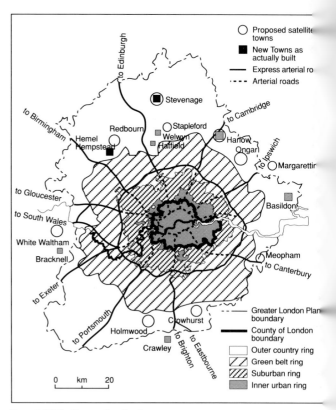

Figure 2.13 The Abercrombie plan for Greater London, 1944

This influential plan argued for the massive decentralisation of population from the inner more congested parts of London's inner boroughs, to the outer rings of London's hinterland. In order to prevent the building of yet more peripheral housing estates at the edge of the **conurbation**, Abercrombie proposed a 8.5 km wide green belt around London as an effective barrier to further urban sprawl and also to act as a valuable recreational resource for Londoners. The movement of overspill population to beyond this green belt would place it well beyond the normal outer limit of commuting to London at that time. Abercrombie proposed to decant over 1 million people into new satellite settlements, following the principles that Ebenezer Howard had established nearly 50 years before. But apart from the experimental private New Towns at Letchworth and Welwyn, inspired by Howard, there was no previous experience within the existing local government structure to implement such a plan. It was therefore decided to set up special development corporations to oversee the building of each town and then to hand over to local government when the town reached its target population.

The post-war governments of Britain acted on the recommendations of the various reports, not always adopting the plans in their entirety, but always following the main suggestions in essence. Between 1945 and 1952 there was a remarkable burst of legislation, all of it aimed at shaping and managing Britain's urban and industrial landscapes.

1945   The Distribution of Industry Act
1946   The New Towns Act
1947   The Town and Country Planning Act
1949   The National Parks and Access to the
          Countryside Act
1952   The Town Development Act

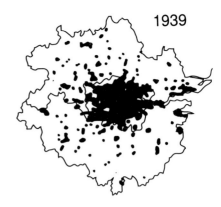

Thus the post-war planning machine was born, the first attempt at comprehensive management of urban change on a national level. Every major conurbation in Britain was the subject of a regional plan but none matched the scope of Abercrombie's plan for London. Professor Peter Hall in *London 2001* describes how Abercrombie rose to the occasion.

'*The point about his plan* (see figure 2.13) *is its extraordinary cartoon-like simplicity, which conceals great subtlety. London, that most chaotic, that least organized of all the world's cities, was at last to have order imposed upon it. But it was to be an organic order: it would arise almost naturally, out of the old London, because it was an order that was lurking just underneath the chaotic surface. London, Abercrombie argued, was – just like the cliché – a collection of villages. They could no longer be recognized; but by building a hierarchy of new arterial and sub-arterial highways, you would not only relieve traffic congestion and make the streets safer, you would also define the edges of London's local communities. And the really major ringways would additionally define critical breaks in London's physical and functional structure: the edge of the central area, the edge of the densely built-up inner Victorian London, the edge of suburbia against open countryside.*'

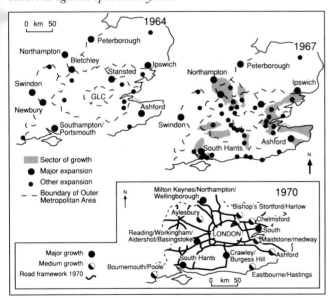

Figure 2.14 Plans for the expansion of the South East

The acknowledgement that London's influence should stretch way beyond the boundaries of Greater London was a major achievement of the plan. It was also a major deterrent to its implementation. This was a *regional* plan (with only advisory powers), but the planning powers created by the 1947 Act were to *local* authorities.

Almost inevitably the local authorities adopted a defensive stance against any strategy which might be deemed detrimental to their own area. Three other factors damaged the plan's strategy.

• *In-migration to London continued unabated in the 1950s and 1960s.*

• *The birth rate rose unexpectedly between 1955 and 1964. Housebuilding forecasts, car ownership predictions, estimates of demands for road space, all had to be revised – upwards!*

• *This growing population began in the 1960s to split into an ever-increasing number of smaller and smaller households. This was the product of social changes such as earlier marriages, the tendency of many young people to leave in search of employment or further education, and an increasing trend for retired people to live by themselves, independent of their families. Predictions of the character and size of housing demands, in particular in inner London comprehensive development areas, had to be revised.*

The Government's planning strategies were also revised. Several further regional studies were prepared culminating in the 1970 Strategic Plan for the South East (see figure 2.14), which remains the most important regional planning document since the 1944 Abercrombie Plan. All of these plans struggled to keep up with the pace of socio-economic change in post-war London and the erosion of urban environmental quality appeared to continue unabated (see figure 2.15). Therefore the plans and the process of strategic planning were deemed to be failures. It is worthwhile, however, pausing to list some of the achievements of the Abercrombie Plan and its successors and to briefly examine the characteristics of the ideal regional city which was their aim (see figure 2.16).

• *By 1951 some eight New Town projects had been initiated in the South East region to move people and industry away from London.*

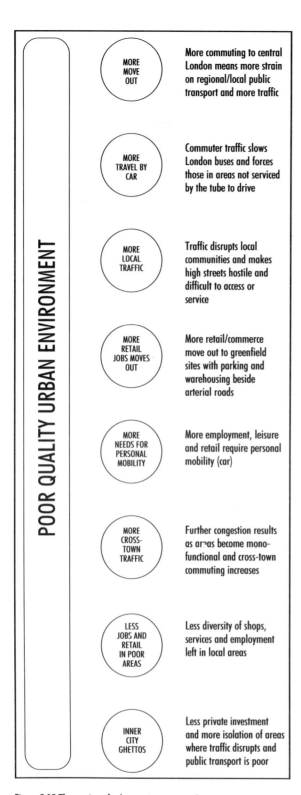

POOR QUALITY URBAN ENVIRONMENT

MORE MOVE OUT — More commuting to central London means more strain on regional/local public transport and more traffic

MORE TRAVEL BY CAR — Commuter traffic slows London buses and forces those in areas not serviced by the tube to drive

MORE LOCAL TRAFFIC — Traffic disrupts local communities and makes high streets hostile and difficult to access or service

MORE RETAIL JOBS MOVES OUT — More retail/commerce move out to greenfield sites with parking and warehousing beside arterial roads

MORE NEEDS FOR PERSONAL MOBILITY — More employment, leisure and retail require personal mobility (car)

MORE CROSS-TOWN TRAFFIC — Further congestion results as areas become mono-functional and cross-town commuting increases

LESS JOBS AND RETAIL IN POOR AREAS — Less diversity of shops, services and employment left in local areas

INNER CITY GHETTOS — Less private investment and more isolation of areas where traffic disrupts and public transport is poor

Figure 2.15 The erosion of urban environment quality

- *Many existing towns had also been identified for large-scale expansion to accommodate the outward movement of industries and their associated overspill population. These new and expanded towns proved singularly successful and demonstrated that good living conditions and a higher quality of environment could be achieved by careful land use planning (see figure 2.18).*

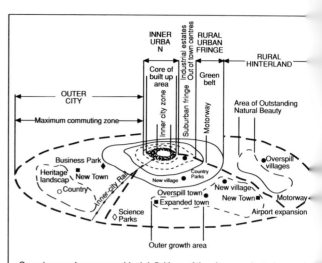

Superimposed on geographical definitions of the city are selected examples of different kinds of planned change. The rural-urban fringe and rural hinterland around the central city provides space for new motorways which run through the green belt. The limits of the outer commuting zone are set by transport improvements in railway and road networks and the costs of journey to work. Public projects such as motorways, airports and New Towns stimulate the demand for private sector developments e.g. investment in housing, industry, commercial and retail enterprises, which in turn encourage population and employment decentralisation.

Figure 2.16 The ideal regional city or metropolis

Figure 2.17 New Town environment, Milton Keynes

Figure 2.18 London green belt buffer zone, Hertfordshire

The establishment of the metropolitan green belt confirmed that it was possible to restrict the growth of London (see figure 2.19).

Many of the plans' proposals were incorporated in the development plans prepared by the local planning authorities in the London Metropolitan Region (LMR) and parts of the rest of South East England (RoSE). The London County Council (LCC), for example, designated 13 Comprehensive Development Areas (CDAs) covering over 500 ha (see figure 2.19). By acquiring land compulsorily, the provision of basic social services, transport services, and housing supply could be facilitated. Even better, these services could be planned ahead of development and provision made for them.

93 per cent of the 172 000 planning applications which were processed each year between 1947 and 1965 were approved. This gives some indication of the rate of development and presumably most, if not all, the successful applications complied with the zoning proposals in the development plans.

- Above all, the plans provided clear and positive guidance about the role of the metropolis, the relationship of town and country, the redevelopment of Inner London, and the promotion of a green belt to restrain the peripheral growth of London.

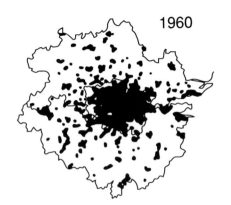

1960

Figure 2.19 The Isle of Dogs, a Comprehensive Development Area of London

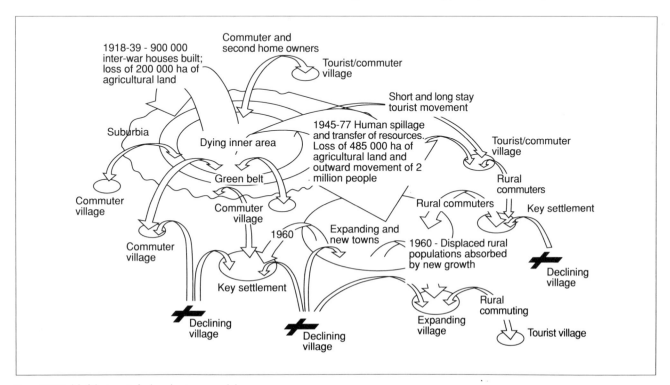

Figure 2.20 Model of the impact of urban planning on rural change

It was inevitable that such far-reaching proposals would have their problems, but it was surprising how quickly the aspirations of the population outpaced and diverged from the aims of the planners and the government. The failures or perceived failures were fairly obvious. London continued to fail to meet its housing needs, to open up its overcrowded areas, to ease congestion, to ameliorate the effects of the decline in manufacturing, and to provide the high quality urban experience which the politicians continually promised.

Perhaps unfairly then the strategic planning process was discredited. A system which purported to be saving agricultural land and South East England's rural heritage was perceived to be failing in its task. The problems had simply been spread outwards, not solved. The degree of impact on rural change seemed to have been underestimated (see figure 2.20). However, if anything it was the power of the knee jerk reaction of the NIMBYs which had been underestimated.

In 1979 the newly elected Conservative Government pledged to reduce State intervention and enhance the role of the private sector. This Government was committed to effecting radical change to the post-war Welfare State. The machinery for managing urban development remained much the same as before (see figure 2.21). The planning system was still the most effective tool for environmental management available to the Departments of State (see figure 2.22). There was however a subtle shift of emphasis. Demand-led planning was now the order of the day. Privatisation, deregulation, and private-public sector partnerships were now very much to the fore. Local government became more reactionary, regulating development initiated by the private sector in response to market forces, rather than being pro-active and promoting their own vision of how the social and material environment of different places should be developed. Planners, as one commentator put it, had been put in their place!

The advisory role of the regional plans also changed. Designated local authority associations – the London Planning Advisory Committee (LPAC) within London, and the Standing Conference for South East Regional Planning (SERPLAN) for the whole of the South East area – now provide official advice to the Government, who respond by issuing regional guidance. The latter provides firm guidance to the local planning authorities in drawing up their own local plans which are now called Unitary Development Plans.

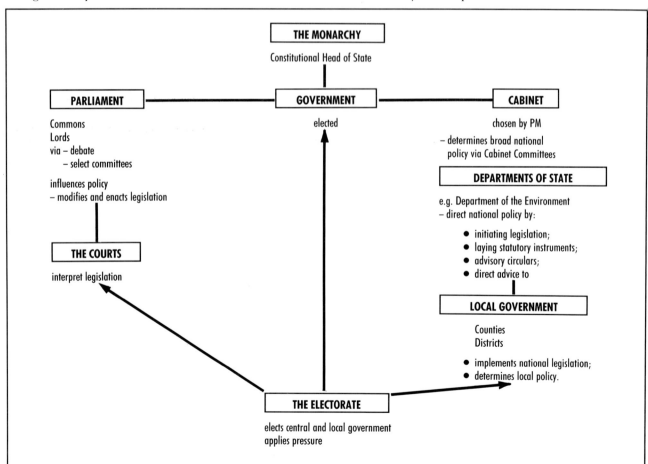

Figure 2.21 British policy-making, 1988

Economic regeneration was reaffirmed as the main aim but less emphasis was given to measures involving public spending with increased priority to involving private investors and the voluntary sector in urban renewal. The urban riots of 1981 did lead to small increases in public expenditure but it was somewhat ironic that at the same time the government were cutting back on mainstream grants to local authorities as well as restricting the amount of money that they could raise themselves through local rates.

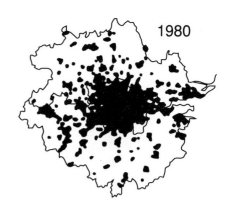
1980

DEPARTMENTS OF STATE: WHO'S RESPONSIBLE FOR WHAT?

Department of the Environment
- Physical (land use) planning carried out by local authorities;
- housing;
- inner cities;
- New Towns and Urban Development Corporations;
- countryside planning, environmental protection and water supply;
- local government and the administration of council finances.

Department of Transport
- Road, rail and air infrastructure;
- building motorways and trunk roads and supervising the allocation of grants to local authorities (County Councils) for local spending on roads;
- Channel Tunnel.

Department of Trade and Industry
- Industrial regeneration;
- manufacturing and service industries;
- high technology;
- the location of industrial development through regional policies and the Regional Development Grant.

Department of Employment
- Education
- Employment and training policy;
- economic planning, small businesses, development of tourism;
- Manpower Services Commission – responsible for employment centres and mobility of labour.

Department of Energy
- Investment plans of nationalised industries;
- siting of nuclear power stations;
- oil drilling installations;
- coal mining developments.

Ministry of Defence
- Location and size of services bases, reservation of training grounds;
- research establishments.

Ministry of Agriculture, Fisheries and Food
- Farm prices and crop support quotas, upland hill farm subsidies;
- reclamation of moorland and lowland.

Figure 2.22 Departments of Stateß who's responsible for what?

SOME 'OUTSTANDING' MANAGEMENT PROBLEMS

• **The inability of London to meet its housing needs.** London's population is in a continuous state of flux. Housing needs vary according to a person's age, stage in the family cycle, and employment status and location. In Greater London as a whole there were almost 2.8 million dwellings in 1986. Two-thirds of these are in the private sector and one-third in the public sector. Eighty per cent of the public sector housing is owned by the London local authorities. The eight boroughs with the highest percentage of local authority housing within them form a continuous arc from Islington, Hackney and Tower Hamlets across the Thames to Greenwich, Lewisham, Southwark, and Lambeth (see figure 2.23). Broadly speaking the inner boroughs provided public housing to replace the existing slums and to ease the high population densities. The fast growing suburbs in outer London were created mainly by the private sector. During the 1950s and 1960s slum clearance became a priority, but this time the preferred style of public housing was often the industrialised high-rise block of flats which in turn led to problems of their own. Many of the high-rise flats were poorly designed and badly built. By the 1970s a reaction against wholesale slum clearance had taken place and housing

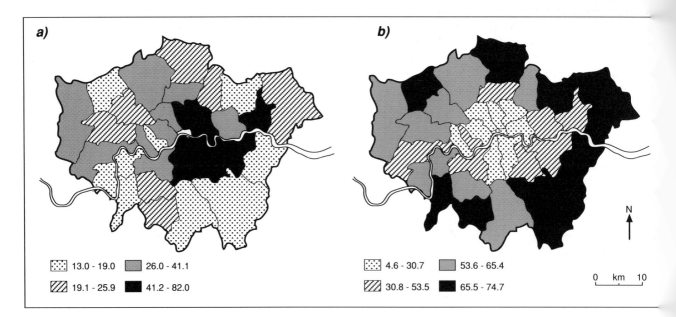

a)

b)

13.0 - 19.0　　26.0 - 41.1

19.1 - 25.9　　41.2 - 82.0

4.6 - 30.7　　53.6 - 65.4

30.8 - 53.5　　65.5 - 74.7

N

0　km　10

Figure 2.23 a) Percentage of households renting from the local authority, 1981

b) Percentage of owner occupier households, 1981

Figure 2.24 The Ronan Point disaster in 1968 focused the disillusionment of high-rise tenants everywhere

improvement, which is cheaper and less damaging to communities, became the preferred option (see figure 2.24).

Gentrification is another trend which has caused pressure on the housing stock. Many delapidated working class areas have been 'invaded' by the middle classes who value the central position of the inner city fringe. Once this process has started the original occupiers are often displaced due to rising property prices and the whole social character of the area is changed.

The quality of the housing stock available is also a problem. In certain problem estates nearly one-third of the total housing stock is deemed to be difficult to let. Professor Alice Coleman highlighted the problems caused by design disadvantagement.

As can be seen in figure 2.25 all the disadvantagements increased as the number of storeys increased. But do tall buildings cause crime? The increasing number of inadequately housed people, and the spread of homelessness was also a growing cause for concern. The inner boroughs which had the longest house waiting lists were compelled to pay for bed and breakfast accommodation in order to meet their obligations to the homeless. Some extra funding was provided by the government in 1989 in an attempt to ease the reliance on this discredited system. The homeless

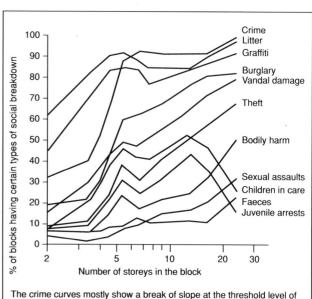

The crime curves mostly show a break of slope at the threshold level of three storeys and thereafter rise more steeply. Families with children are regarded as not at risk in walk-up blocks without lifts and in high-rise buildings

Figure 2.25 Social breakdown and height of tower block

...ung people who inhabit the now familiar **...rdboard cities** at either end of Charing Cross ...ilway station, only serve to highlight the growing ...equality in incomes of Londoners which ...xacerbates the housing problem at every level.

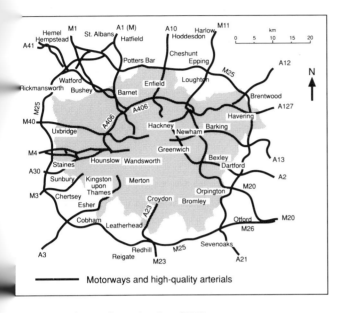

Figure 2.26 London's road network in the mid-1990s

Motorways and high-quality arterials

- **Transport problems** make or break cities. Abercrombie's plan suggested an outer metropolitan ring route around the **suburban** fringe of Greater London in 1944. The completion of the M25 in 1986 finally saw this part of his plan fulfilled. The plan's ideal of using motorways or major arterial routes as barriers denoting changes in land use proved very popular. Abercrombie's idea of using roads to delimit neighbourhoods and thus give them a greater sense of community was used in many urban areas – but not in London. So when the orbital M25 was built it attracted large numbers of radial commuters, who used the orbital motorway to gain access to less busy radials, something the planners had not thought of. A glance at London's present road system reveals glaring gaps (see figure 2.26). The system provides unequal access to different parts of London and the South East. Abercrombie's major radial arterial routes have simply never been built. Whatever the method of travel, central London journey speeds have remained almost constant throughout this century. This is partly due to the inherited structure and the inability of new technologies to either adapt to the inherited quagmire of communications or to obliterate it. Mismanagement and lack of co-ordination are also to blame. Thanks to an Act of

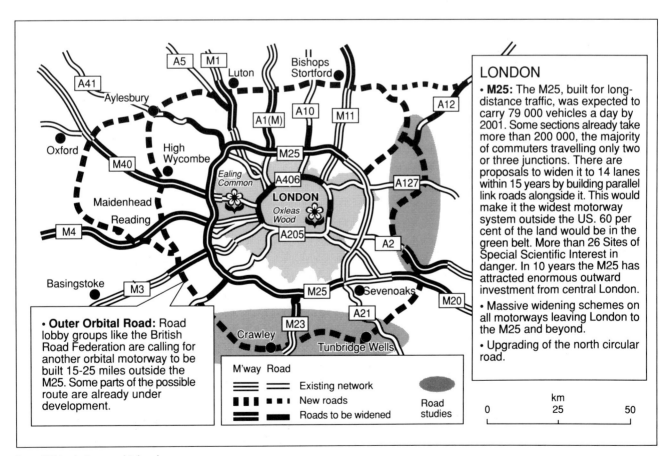

LONDON

- **M25:** The M25, built for long-distance traffic, was expected to carry 79 000 vehicles a day by 2001. Some sections already take more than 200 000, the majority of commuters travelling only two or three junctions. There are proposals to widen it to 14 lanes within 15 years by building parallel link roads alongside it. This would make it the widest motorway system outside the US. 60 per cent of the land would be in the green belt. More than 26 Sites of Special Scientific Interest in danger. In 10 years the M25 has attracted enormous outward investment from central London.
- Massive widening schemes on all motorways leaving London to the M25 and beyond.
- Upgrading of the north circular road.

- **Outer Orbital Road:** Road lobby groups like the British Road Federation are calling for another orbital motorway to be built 15-25 miles outside the M25. Some parts of the possible route are already under development.

M'way Road
Existing network
New roads
Roads to be widened
Road studies

Figure 2.27 London's outer orbital road

25

Parliament in 1846, no main line railways were allowed to enter or cross central London. This ensured that as London's suburbs spread, commuters would still have to walk to work, having been dumped on the edge of the CBD. It was this ban which led to the birth of underground railways. The Metropolitan and District lines of the 1860s were joined together into the Circle Line in the 1880s, and were then followed by the deep-level tubes in the 1890s. The underground was so successful that it was extended in the 1920s and 1930s above ground and was responsible for that vast world of semi-detached housing that spread out from the suburban stations in the inter-war years, the sprawl which John Betjeman immortalised in *Metro-land* quoted from below.

> *Funereal from Harrow draws the train,*
> *On, on, northwestwards, London far away,*
> *And stations start to look quite countrified.*
> *Pinner, a parish of a thousand souls,*
> *Til the railways gave it many thousands more.*

Heathrow airport has repeated the underground's success in generating development, but otherwise there has been an inadequate response to the all too evident deficiencies in the transport system.

- *Construction has failed to keep up with traffic demands even in areas where most commuters are car dependent.*
- *The outer commuter services, and the inner commuter services south of the Thames, fail to directly serve central London destinations.*
- *The lack of orbital services inhibits development. Americans in particular are astounded by London's lack of orbital roads or 'beltways' as they call them, although there are plans to remedy this situation (see figure 2.27).*
- *The whole system lacks coherence. For example, there is no plan to develop park and ride stations. Road and rail investments should be complementary rather than competitive.*

POLICY SHIFT

'Nothing should be allowed to come in the way of the great car economy.'
Margaret Thatcher, prime minister, 1979

'I will not allow Britain's first-rate businesses to be disadvantaged by a second-rate road network.'
Paul Channon, transport minister, 1988

'There are some who argue that expansion of the road network will be devastating for the environment. They are wrong …'
John MacGregor, transport minister, 1992

'I love cars of all shapes and sizes. Cars are a good thing. I also love roads. I have always loved roads. If ever there was an environmentally unfriendly form of transport, it was railways.'
Robert Key, roads minister, 1994

'Our priority now must be to make the most effective use of the existing network … and building to remove congestion and blackspots.'
Brian Mawhinney, transport minister, 1994

Figure 2.28 Policy shift?

In this time of demand-led planning the slippage on major transport link improvements may seem surprising, but it is the huge financial sums involved which tend to slow the process up and which have led to interesting changes in emphasis from the politicians involved (see figure 2.28).

- **Managing economic change** has also proved difficult. London's economy generates plenty of good well-paying jobs but also a host of poorly-paid ones and no jobs at all for a substantial minority of its population.

Sector	Employment	Britain %	RoSE %	Greater London %
0	Agriculture, forestry, fisheries	1	2	0
1	Energy, water	2	1	1
2	Metal manufacturing, chemicals	3	3	1
3	Metal goods engineering	10	10	5
4	Other manufacture	9	7	7
5	Construction	4	4	3
61–3, 66–7	Wholesale distribution, hotels	11	11	10
64–5	Retail distribution	10	11	9
7	Transport and communications	6	6	9
8	Banking, insurance, finance	12	13	22
91–2	Public administration, and defence	9	8	11
93–9	Education, health, other	22	24	22

Figure 2.29 Employment structure of Britain, Greater London and the Rest of the South East, 1991

The most conspicuous single trend in London's economy over the past 25 years has been the shift out of manufacturing into services (see figures 2.11 and 2.29). This deindustrialisation mirrors the nation-wide trend but is even more exaggerated in the capital city, where the massive loss of jobs in manufacturing has been accompanied by a decentralisation of jobs from London's core to its outer rings. Unfortunately the increase in service sector jobs has not kept pace with the losses, even in the all too short economic upturn of the late 1980s (see figure 2.30). The role of the office in keeping London's economy buoyant cannot be overstressed. London is pre-eminent as Britain's office centre, with nearly one-third of national office employment and almost 40 per cent of commercial floor space. Offices have been built speculatively in every post-war office boom that London has experienced. The most recent office building boom of the late 1980s has left an excess supply of available property and hence a slackening demand as reflected in static or declining rents and higher vacancy rates. Despite empty offices and declining rents London remains to be one of the world's three main financial centres. London has continued to attract tourists and new investment, and to earn revenue around the world, but it is fairly obvious that the city's comparative advantage has been eroded. There is now a severe

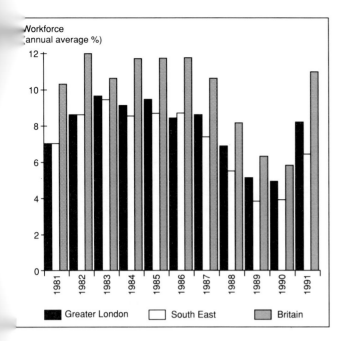

Figure 2.30 Unemployment in Britain, Greater London and the South East in 1992

shortage of skilled labour which is a disadvantage to the firms in Greater London which are trying to adjust to global competition. Such competition is critical. Today's international or trans-global companies can switch investment away from high costs areas more easily than in the past. Growing international competition has also raised the pace of technological innovation, which in turn has favoured more modern, spacious factories and larger offices specially designed for the latest computer and telecommunications equipment. Managing such a pace of change requires vision – the same vision which gave London the first underground railway in the world, the first modern integrated transport corporation combining buses, trains and trolley buses, and a public housing system which was a model for so many others. London now has a more fragmented city government than any other major competing city and required vision will be hard to find.

The changes in London's employment structure are regarded as a major determinant of changes in social structure. London is becoming a city of parts, some wealthy and healthy, others not, under the influence of the following trends.

- *Growth in professional and managerial secure and well-paid jobs.*
- *Underpinned by growth in supporting service employment of which a minority is secure and well-paid and a majority is insecure and poorly-paid.*
- *Decline in well-paid skilled manual jobs.*
- *Increases in the black economy and the unemployed.*

- **Inner London urban renewal** is another pressing problem to address. As we have already seen, the Comprehensive Development Area policy was not entirely successful. The employment, environmental and often ethnic hardships which are commonly referred to as inner city problems, remain part of London's urban landscape. A whole range of strategies exist to assist the regeneration of the whole inner city. The main aims are: to enhance job prospects and the ability of residents to compete for them; to bring land and buildings back into use; to encourage private sector investment; to improve housing conditions; and to encourage self help and improve the social fabric.

The strategies in use include:

- *Urban Programme Grants are given to inner city local authorities in order to encourage enterprise, improve derelict sites, and upgrade council housing (see figure 2.31).*

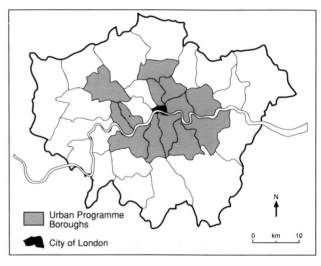

Figure 2.31 Urban programme authorities eligible for additional government grants in London

- *City Action Teams and Task Forces aim to secure improved co-operation between government departments in inner cities and to encourage partnerships between business, local and central government, the voluntary sector, and the local inhabitants.*
- *Urban Development Corporations (UDCs) started in 1981 with the establishment of the London (and Merseyside) Docklands UDCs. The principal aim is to speed up private sector investment in derelict urban sites by short circuiting the planning process and acquiring land compulsorily, if necessary.*
- *Enterprise Zones (EZs) were introduced in 1980 with the aim of stimulating industrial and commercial activity by removing certain tax burdens and relaxing planning controls. Various financial incentives, geared towards property development, are available in EZs such as the Isle of Dogs.*

11 Explain and discuss the strength of reaction against urban sprawl around London.

12 Outline the proposals of the 1945 Greater London Plan to contain this urban sprawl.

13 Comment on the various impacts on the area surrounding London of the decentralisation strategies adopted after the 1939–45 war (see figure 2.26).

14 Outline the problems which eventually discredited high-rise blocks of flats as a major method of housing improvement.

15 Le Corbusier, Ebenezer Howard, Frank Lloyd Wright and Patrick Geddes were all important urban theorists whose ideas permeate urban management to this day. Choose one of these figures and research their main ideas, outlining their importance to urban management today.

16 Dr Janice Perlman of New York University has stated that 'every first-world city has within it a third-world city of malnutrition, infant mortality, homelessness, and unemployment. And conversely, every third-world city has within it a first-world city of high tech, high fashion, and high finance.'
   Discuss this statement with reference to present-day London.

The London Docklands

The strategic planning style no longer dominates urban management in Britain as it did from 1945–79. The 1980s and 1990s have witnessed the emergence of a new emphasis, not merely in Britain, but world-wide, on the planning of large-scale individual projects – mega-projects. The Glasgow Eastern Area Renewal of the 1970s shared the same aims but, in terms of scale, there really has been no British precedent for the reconstruction of London Docklands (see figures 2.32, 2.33 and 2.34). The Docklands have been on a dramatic economic roller coaster ride since the construction of the first enclosed wet docks in the 1790s. The suddenness of the closures, even after the process had started in 1967 with the closure of the East India Docks, took everyone by surprise. With the benefit of hindsight it can be seen that a variety of problems quietly and insidiously engulfed the area from 1900 onwards. London lost 1.5 million people between its 1939 peak and 1977 and 500 000 manufacturing jobs between 1961 and 1971.

Containerisation expanded the roll-on/roll-off ferries on the English Channel and East Anglian coasts at the expense of London's Port. The coastal coal trade ceased, while air transport mushroomed. Heathrow airport's value (not volume) of trade overtook that of the Port of London's in the mid-1970s.

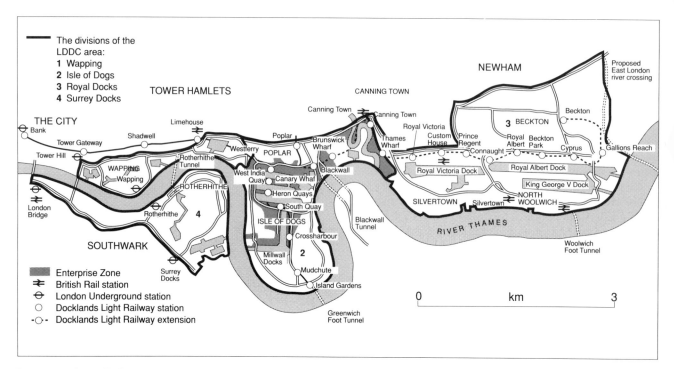

Figure 2.32 London Docklands

Figure 2.33 London Docks before regeneration

Figure 2.34 Canary Wharf, Docklands

One by one the great docks closed, taking with them the related ship repair, marine engineering, transport services, and a whole range of industries which had originally established themselves on the waterfront as part of the docks' great entrepôt agglomeration. The wasteland created, exceeded even the damage caused by the Luftwaffe in the 1939–45 war. The trading centre of Empire and Commonwealth fell eerily silent (see figure 2.33).

During the 1970s various ideas, proposals and projects came and went. The most promising of these efforts, the London Docklands Strategic Plan (1976), aimed to redress the imbalance between East and West London, aiming to meet local needs, and promote a partnership between the three tiers of local government. The age of strategic planning drew to a close with the incoming Conservative Government of 1979. Within weeks, Michael Heseltine, the newly appointed Secretary of State for the Environment, announced his intention to establish Urban Development Corporations (UDCs) to oversee the redevelopment of the London Docklands and Merseyside docks area.

The London Docklands Development Corporation's (LDDC's) area comprises some 2100 ha, taking in parts of the three East London boroughs of Tower Hamlets, Newham and Southwark (see figure 2.32). The LDDC's objectives are to: *'redevelop its area by investment in reclamation and infrastructure, together with business and community support for residential and commercial development. By co-operating with other authorities, the area will become an increasingly pleasant and rewarding place in which to live, work and play.'*

The LDDC also manages the Isle of Dogs Enterprise Zone established in 1982. This now famous tongue of land enclosed by a meander of the Thames has been the site of some of the most rapid and speculative development that London has seen. The achievements of this *laissez-faire* strategy (anything goes!) are fairly obvious.

- *The centre of gravity of the city has been perceptibly moved eastwards. By 1988 around 13 000 homes had been built, 1.6 million m^2 of commercial development had been completed, a new light railway was in operation, a new airport was functioning and some 28 000 new jobs had been created.*
- *The population decline, characteristic of inner city degeneration, has not only been halted but has been reversed. The population of Docklands has doubled since the early 1980s.*
- *The speed of the development has been spectacular. Large tracts of derelict urban land have been rehabilitated and in the process the entire image of the area has been transformed. Docklands is now a major tourist attraction.*
- *The development has succeeded in maintaining its private sector emphasis. By 1988 an expenditure of £440 million of public money had levered ten times that amount of private investment – £4440 million.*
- *The infrastructure is gradually improving. The Docklands Light Railway extension to Beckton opened in 1993 and there are plans to extend the railway south of the Thames to Lewisham in an attempt to provide an alternative route to the City from South East London and at the same time improve access to the Isle of Dogs. The Limehouse Link, a four-lane tunnel connecting the City to the Isle of Dogs, is now complete. At around £170 million for just over 1.7 km of roadway it has been dubbed* 'the most expensive road in the world'.

In terms of physical regeneration and investment, London Docklands is an outstanding success. However, there is still a long way to go before the dream of Docklands joining with the twin cores of the City of London and the City of Westminster, to become London's third city, is fulfilled. There are a few problems to be solved.

- *The largest office scheme in Docklands, Canary Wharf, is continuing to attract new tenants but at a slower rate than anticipated. London office workers still perceive Canary Wharf as a fearsomely difficult place to commute to. When BZW, the investment bank, decided to relocate in Canary Wharf in August 1995, the company softened the blow with an extra £1000 payment to each of its employees every year until the Jubilee Line extension opens in 1998.*
- *The new jobs attracted into the area have not solved the problem of rising long-term unemployment. These were in newspapers, TV studios, and financial services with large-scale redevelopment for offices and their headquarters. But such employment is more often than not simply a transfer from elsewhere in metropolitan London. These specialised jobs in publishing, retailing, banking and finance were often unattainable to local people, and training initiatives, designed to help local residents and school leavers to share the incoming jobs, were set up. However, by 1995, with a huge number of unlet offices on offer at fiercely competitive rates, developers' attentions were beginning to turn to leisure, entertainment, culture and education as other possible catalysts for social and economic regeneration.*
- *The capabilities of the existing and planned transport schemes are woefully inadequate. Inaccessibility is proving to be a major deterrent to further development in the area. The extention of the Jubilee Line underground railway link, the proposed East London River Crossing, various extensions to the Docklands Light Railway, the upgrading of the A13, will all help. Critics, however, claim that such improvements should have been in place before, or at least contemporaneously with, the housing and office developments.*

These problems serve as a reminder that there is no quick fix for urban regeneration. Just as cities do not decline overnight, neither can they be nursed instantaneously back to health. Setting up a UDC for only five to seven years is extremely short-sighted practice. The time required for environmental change is extremely long and that for social regeneration is even longer.

London Docklands has provided a critical mass of office development as well as ample housing for the incoming highly-skilled workforce. It should be an unqualified success and yet it is not. To find out why, one need only compare it with the **Edge Cities** which have proliferated in the United States in recent years. Infrastructure, accessibility, communications and that most precious of urban commodities – mobility, are the missing essentials.

Docklands is a classic example of a development which is not supported by the appropriate infrastructure. Only limited investment in roads was made and the low capacity Docklands Light Railway did not even link the docks area with the **Central Business District** (CBD) of London for the first four years of its life. The underground railway map was eventually redrawn in July 1991 when the Bank extension was opened. But the scale of investment simply does not match up to the amount of development which has taken place in Docklands. It is only to be hoped that the same mistake will not be made with the next mega-project.

17 Outline the strategy employed by the London Docklands Development Corporation in order to encourage development in East London.

18 Explain the reasons for the numerous protests by the local population against the activities of the LDDC.

19 Outline the advantages and disadvantages of the LDDC's activities so far under the headings of: jobs; housing; and transport.
  Discuss this statement with reference to present-day London.

SUMMARY

- LONDON REMAINED A COMPACT, DENSELY POPULATED CITY UNTIL THE NINETEENTH CENTURY WHEN TECHNOLOGICAL IMPROVEMENTS IN TRANSPORT SEVERED THE LINK BETWEEN HOME AND WORK.
- LONDON SHARED IN THE ECONOMIC AND SOCIAL UPHEAVAL ASSOCIATED WITH THE INDUSTRIAL REVOLUTION DESPITE HAVING TO IMPORT ALL ITS BULKY RAW MATERIALS. LONDON BECAME AN IMPORTANT BREAK OF BULK POINT.
- LONDON'S URBAN FABRIC WAS LARGELY MANAGED BY ARCHITECTS AND THE BUILDING REGULATIONS UNTIL UNCONFINED URBAN SPRAWL WAS COMBINED WITH CONCERN OVER THE DETERIORATING HEALTH, AMENITY AND CONVENIENCE OF THE URBAN ENVIRONMENT. THIS THEN LED TO THE DEVELOPMENT OF A COMPREHENSIVE PLANNING SYSTEM, WHICH GAVE REGIONAL AND LOCAL AUTHORITIES THE POWER TO DRAW UP PLANNING STRATEGIES.
- LONDON HAS UNDERGONE DRAMATIC ECONOMIC AND SOCIAL CHANGE, THE SPEED OF WHICH HAS SOMETIMES LEFT THE CITY'S URBAN PLANNERS FLOUNDERING IN ITS WAKE.
- IN AN EFFORT TO SPEED UP THE PLANNING PROCESS THERE HAS BEEN A RECENT SWING TOWARDS A LESS PRESCRIPTIVE FORM OF GOVERNMENT INTERVENTION AND A GREATER RELIANCE ON PRIVATE SECTOR INITIATIVES.

3 CASE STUDY: KARACHI

Pakistan: Population Growth and Urbanisation

Understanding the current urban processes at work in an area requires a review of the past. This applies equally to Less Economically Developing Countries (LEDCs) and More Economically Developing Countries (MEDCs), even though the time-scales of urbanisation may vary enormously. This case study considers an area of the Indian sub-continent which has seen the development of urban living from its earliest beginnings.

The present-day boundaries of Pakistan contain the locations of the oldest urban settlements in the Indian sub-continent (see figure 3.1) of which Harappa and Mohenjo Daro are the best known.

This civilisation, based on the agricultural potential of the Indus basin, dates back to 3000 BC, with urban development at its peak from 2000 to 1700 BC. The subsequent disappearance, for 1000 years, of any record of this phase of urbanisation is amongst the earliest examples of the cyclical nature of the process.

POPULATION GROWTH IN PAKISTAN

It is vital to set the urbanisation process against the background of the country's overall population growth (see figure 3.2).

The time-scale employed here is skewed towards the post-colonial era, simply because of the availability and greater accuracy of census data obtained for the area. The first full census of India

Year	Population (millions)	Urban	(%)
1901	16.58	1.62	9.8
1911	19.38	1.69	8.7
1921	21.11	2.06	9.8
1931	23.54	2.77	11.8
1941	28.28	4.02	14.2
1951	33.78	6.02	17.8
1961	42.88	9.65	22.5
1971	64.89	17.04	26.3
1981	102.50	29.60	28.8
1990	122.70	35.40	29.6
1994	126.40	40.44	32.0

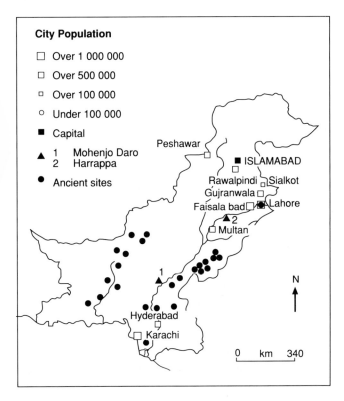

Figure 3.1 Urban centres in Pakistan

Figure 3.2 Population growth in Pakistan, 1901–1994

(which at that time included present-day Pakistan) took place in 1871. Wherever possible, the figures for Pakistan are projected back to allow a clearer picture to emerge. One of the most significant trends is that Pakistan is one of the few countries in Asia with a population growth rate as high as 3 per cent per annum.

From figure 3.2 it is also clear that, while the urban population of Pakistan is only around 30 per cent of the total at present, the growth rate of this urban population is running at a higher rate than the overall growth rate for the country. This provides statistical evidence for the process of increasing urbanisation.

URBANISATION IN PAKISTAN

Thus while there is evidence of urbanisation, it is important to try to understand the causes of the process, and to look at the results in terms of the effects on the people and their country.

The root causes of urbanisation lie predominantly in the rural areas, where the 'push' factors drive increasing numbers of people, both seasonally and permanently, to find employment and accommodation in the cities. Many of Karachi's immigrants are in fact itinerant agricultural workers who come into the city when they cannot find employment on farms in the surrounding area. Eventually, and especially during prolonged periods of drought, many will settle permanently in the City, thus swelling the numbers in the *katchi abadis* (**squatter settlements**). In order to stem the flow of migrants, it is necessary for the Government to address the problems farmers face in the rural hinterland and to seek to establish alternative means of employment in suitable industries.

The results of increasing urbanisation are clear in the cities themselves, where perpetual change and burgeoning population complicate an already difficult management situation for the politicians and planners. Despite the problems existing in LEDCs' cities, these areas continue to exert a powerful attraction for those seeking a way out of the poverty and misery of the rural areas. Obviously many 'pull' factors continue to operate. These include the potential for employment and the expectation of some sort of accommodation, which all too often fail to materialise.

As is shown in the next section, the planners in Karachi have been forced to accept the continued existence of squatter settlements, to manage their improvement and control their development, rather than try to remove them altogether. In this experience, Karachi exhibits characteristics which are very similar to those in many other developing cities.

1 **Compare the figures for Pakistan's total population and urban population over the ten-year period shown in figure 3.3, and briefly try to account for the differences.**

	Total population (million)	% growth	Urban population (million)	% growth
1981	100	3.0	30	5.0
1991	110	3.1	40	7.0

Figure 3.3 Pakistan's urban growth

2 **From the figures provided in Figure 3.4, construct a Rank Order table for each statistic.**

	Population (million)	% growth	% urban
India	911.6	1.9	26
Pakistan	126.4	3.0	28
Bangladesh	116.6	2.4	14
Sri Lanka	17.9	1.5	22
Afghanistan	17.8	2.8	18

Figure 3.4 Urban population in selected countries in Asia, 1994

3 **Comment on the results of Question 2, with particular reference to Pakistan.**

4 **Look at figure 3.5. It gives two different predictions for Pakistan's future population growth. Which prediction do you think is likely to occur? Give reasons for your answer.**

	Total population (million)	% growth	Urban population (million)	% growth
A?	125	3.0	55	8.0
B?	115	2.5	50	7.0

Figure 3.5 Population in Pakistan, predictions for 2001

Karachi: Growth and Structure

Karachi is situated on the shores of the Arabian Sea, to the north of the mouth of the River Indus (see figure 3.7). It is a relatively young city with only a small fishing village at the mouth of the Lyari River, and a fortification at Manora up until the early part of the nineteenth century.

In 1839, the fort was taken by the British, who then began the development of the modern City inland from the original coastal village. They dredged and improved the natural harbour, and laid out a street plan in the area between the Lyari and Malir Rivers, thus beginning the landward

When the new state was created, the capital was established in Karachi, though this was to move to Islamabad in 1971. However, the initial impetus this gave to the commercial and industrial life of Karachi ensured that it quickly became the largest and most important city in Pakistan with the largest port, a major international airport, main rail and road termini and a wide variety of industries. The Metropolitan Area now houses 6 per cent of Pakistan's total population and 22 per cent of its urban population. It generates 15 per cent of the nation's gross domestic product (GDP), and accounts for 35 per cent of employment in large-scale manufacturing.

Karachi's rapid population growth can be seen in figure 3.8. Most of the current growth stems from immigrants from the surrounding agricultural hinterland, or from farther afield in Pakistan.

xpansion of the City which has continued to the present day.

Partly due to its strategic importance, and also because it was cooler than the original capital at Hyderabad, Karachi became the capital of Sind province in 1843. With the expansion of the City railway system in the 1860s and continued improvements to the now bustling harbour (the Karachi Port Trust was established in 1887), its commercial and industrial future was assured, despite the economic dominance held by Bombay throughout this period up to the creation of the state of Pakistan in 1947.

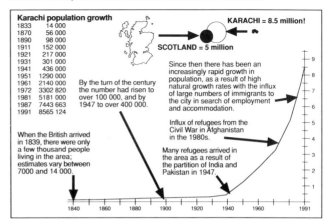

Figure 3.8 Karachi: population growth

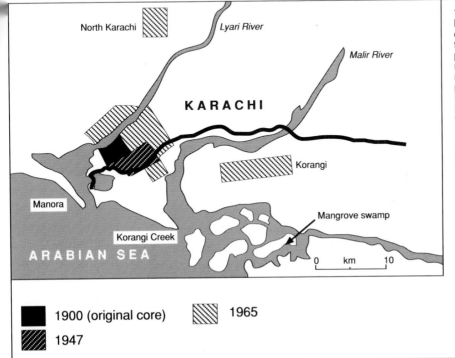

1947
By independence in 1947 considerable expansion had occurred to the east of the original centre. This was linked to port development and the growth of the railways connecting Karachi with the rest of the Indian sub-continent. The provision of paved roads and streets lagged far behind, and played little part in the direction of physical growth of the town.

1965
By 1965 improvements to the road network, though patchy and often poorly planned, had begun to be felt, and the city had expanded in all directions.
Two main areas of expansion can be noted.
1 The townships of Korangi and Landhi (both established next to new industrial areas) far to the east of the centre.
2 North Karachi.
These were early attempts to remove people from some of the slums in the city and provide them with better houses, services and jobs about 17 km from the centre. Unfortunately most who moved there were forced to continue working in the central area, and many tried to return to houses nearer their jobs rather than commute this distance.

Figure 3.7 Karachi: early growth

However, many previously arrived in the area as refugees from India, as a result of the partition of the two countries which coincided with Independence from the UK in 1947. As a result, Karachi now has a very mixed population; the Sindis, natives of the region, account for less than 10 per cent of the population; while Pathans, Punjabis, Muhajirs and Baluchis together constitute over 90 per cent.

By the time of the 1991 census, the population had risen to over 8 million, and estimates for the year 2000 are put at over 11 million people.

THE PHYSICAL GROWTH OF KARACHI

The present City of Karachi covers an area of about 150 000 ha. In 1947, the total built-up area was only 18 600 ha, and most of that was due to rapid expansion under the direction of the British colonial administration in the late nineteenth century. The original site consisted largely of a group of islands and sand spits. On the landward side were some barren hillocks, and it was between these and along the shore of the main bay (see figure 3.9) that the early fishing villages grew up.

By the time the British arrived a small walled town had developed in what is now the commercial heart of the City, stretching from Kharadar near the shore to Mithadar on the Lyari River. From this centre expansion has taken place mostly to the north and east. Most of the older public buildings date from the late nineteenth century, during the period of British colonial rule. Indeed, many of the housing areas on the fringe of the Central Business District (CBD) were built to accommodate military personnel and civil servants, and were variously named as 'Barracks', 'Quarters' or 'Lines', names which they retain to this day. In fact the modern Pakistani Army still provides accommodation for its officers in the City in this way.

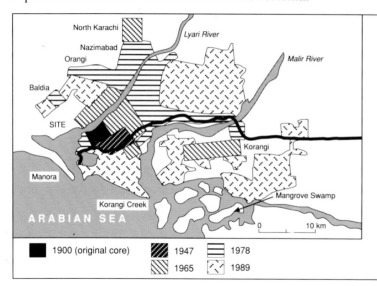

1978
By 1978 further infill had occured, along with a general expansion mostly to the north and east. By this time too, the first developments of the area of Orangi had begun. This is one of the largest of the many Bastis of Karachi, and it consists of a 'legal' area housing about 100 000 people and an 'illegal' area accomodating about 400 000 people. Orangi town and Baldia Colony were the first of the major expansions to the north west of the city; the squatter settlements were pushing out towards a major air base, often following dry water courses, since these are ignored by official housing and commercial developments. This has also occured within the city, and accounts for much of the infill of urban growth around what are usually middle-class housing areas.

1989
Since the mid-1970s the growth of housing has been more directly controlled and planned by the authorities, and attempts have been made to improve and upgrade the squatter settlements. Much of this has occured under the Karachi Master Plan, which was developed and implemented by the Karachi Development Authority in conjunction with the Karachi Metropolitan Corporation, with help from the United Nations as well as other National agencies and authorities within Pakistan.

Figure 3.9 Karachi: modern growth

Figure 3.10 Bus station, Karachi

Figure 3.11 Land to be developed, Karachi

Managing Change in Karachi

Planning decisions and the management of change in a city like Karachi pose particular problems for municipal authorities. The City is growing at a faster rate than the politicians and planners can cope with. The Karachi Development Authority (KDA) has to work in a reactive way. It can make five-year plans but because of a lack of funds and the control to implement the plans they will literally stay on the drawing board. What can be done is to try to regulate what is being created by the informal sector. As much as one-third of Karachi's population live in shanty dwellings with no uniform access to public services. The process of shanty building and service provision is considered in the next section.

Karachi: Squatter Settlements

SHANTY TOWNS: DISEASE OR DEVELOPMENT OPPORTUNITY?

One of the characteristic features of many large cities in developing countries is the existence of large areas of poor quality shanty housing, often on the outskirts of the city, which lack any of the basic amenities such as piped water supplies, sanitation systems or electricity. In Karachi, these are known as *katchi-abadis*. In the 1980s the population of these increased from 25 to 40 per cent of the City population. There are 536 listed *katchi-abadis* with an estimated population of 3 560 800 people, and rising!

They have come into existence partly as a result of the lack of proper urban management and planning, and partly in response to the lack of adequate affordable housing for the poor in the City. The City authority does not have the power to prevent the establishment of such areas.

BRITAIN

PLANNING In a city in Britain the municipal authority will have a highly qualified and well-trained planning department. The city will be divided up into defined areas and Local Plans will be drawn up at regular intervals. These provide a framework for control over land use and management of city growth and guidelines for the provision of services and public utilities. There is always a period of public consultation before a plan is finalised.

BUDGETING The local authority gains its income from direct local taxation (domestic and commercial rates) and grants from Central Government. A huge bureaucracy has been set up to collect these rates and a yearly planned budget is set to provide services for its citizens.

SERVICES The local authority will allocate funds for roads, education, water, building and maintenance of council housing, recreation and sewage, street lighting etc. Public services like the electricity and gas companies will work alongside the council in housing areas allocated by the council planners and built by private companies. There is no unplanned development and provision of public services is uniform in the specific area.

PAKISTAN

In Karachi there are several different bodies which have authority over different aspects of town planning. The KDA has the role of making up the actual plans for the city. In the past they have been given help by the United Nations Development Programme (UNDP). The implementation of the plan is divided between several autonomous city agencies with no clear links. The planning and development control system is fragmented with no effective, area-wide system for controlling development.

A large proportion of city dwellers in Karachi earn low incomes and cannot afford to pay for services which are provided. The bulk of their income will go on food and they cannot afford rent for flats built by the authorities.

They are forced to build shanty dwellings wherever they can and in many cases these have no access to public services. Theoretical physical planning is not linked to the ability to pay for the actual scheme. In one example if a plan by the KDA to upgrade slums in one area over a five-year period had actually been carried out, the total cost would have exceeded the total income for the whole Sind region by five times.

Service provision is not, however, uniform across the City. There are some areas which have access to all amenities such as water, electricity, gas, sewage, garbage collection, educational and health services and others where the people have built their own houses with no links at all to public utilities.

ELECTRICITY Although nearly 85 per cent of Karachi's population is served by electricity most areas suffer from periodic cuts.

WATER Despite improvements over a ten-year period, only 70 per cent of Karachi's 8.5 million residents in 1990 received their water supply via direct connections. The remainder received supply through tankers or stand pipes.

SEWAGE In 1990 only 36.5 per cent of the 537 345 households had direct connections to the sewerage system.

EDUCATION AND HEALTH facilities are distributed unevenly across the City and there are limited affordable options for the poor.

Figure 3.12 Planning, budgeting and services

Figure 3.13 Shanties in Karachi, Pakistan

HOW DO THESE KATCHI-ABADIS DEVELOP?

Figure 3.12 shows that *katchi-abadis* are distributed widely throughout the City area, although there are some concentrations. The Lyari area near Karachi's City centre consists of many older squatter settlements which are now well-established, while the areas around Baldia and Orangi Town are more recent developments in the north western part of the City.

There are basically three ways in which these unauthorised settlements have developed.

1 Illegal Sub-divisions

When the City authorities started to try to restrict the growth of squatter settlements, particularly in the 1960s in Karachi, alternative sites were sought by the settlers who continued to stream into the City. The system of illegal sub-division of State land on the fringe of the City became commonplace. This system revolved around a middleperson (*dallal*), who acquires the occupation of State land by doing deals with local businesses, and then sub-lets plots of land to settlers at prices they are able to pay. The *dallal* also arranges water supplies and protects the residents from eviction until the shanty settlement is so big that it is safe from that threat. The role of the *dallal* and the officials who work with him/her becomes much more important as time passes, since they stand to make money from rents and land speculation. It is in everyone's interest to see that the threat of eviction is lifted, that services are provided and that local problems are solved.

2 Unauthorised Invasions

Many of the earlier *katchi-abadi* settlements in Karachi arose when migrants arrived in groups and occupied plots of vacant land as near as possible to the City centre or their work-place. These settlements are therefore very crowded, unplanned with narrow winding lanes, and are often the first targets of attempts to upgrade or improve squatter settlements. Because of the way in which settlers arrived, people tend to stick together in their clan

---

The Planner

In the 1970s we were besieged by refugees from Afghanistan as well as from rural areas. Because of these people's lack of income and the lack of cheap housing, they were forced to build illegal squatter settlements or katchi-abadis. We regularly had to use the police and demolition squads to clear the illegal dwellings. We could not allow these to develop as in many cases they were on sites set aside for new road developments or offices outlined in our five-year plan. They were a breeding ground for disease and crime, without services like water, electricity and sewage. The houses, being made of reeds, were very unstable and were a real fire risk with the potential of many deaths because of the density of buildings. Our policy has changed now and with the help of planners from the United Nations Development Programme we do regular surveys of the katchi-abadis and work out which ones are worth keeping and would benefit from regularisation and the provision of services. We have to try to use our limited budget to benefit as many people as possible.

The Katchi-Abadi resident

I have just moved into Karachi from a small village 24 km away. I am planning to build a small hut in one of the katchi-abadis. There are lots of open spaces in Karachi. Some are set aside for future development and some, like those along the railways and in dried up river beds, are not big enough or are too dangerous to put real buildings on. My cousin lives in an area called Mohammed Nagar. With the help of a local politician the people there set up their homes in an area of open land. They drew up a map of 72 m² plots and 30 families built reed huts and moved in. Two weeks later the KDA demolition squad appeared with no warning and destroyed 40 huts. Some people left, but most came back and rebuilt their huts as they had nowhere else to go. The demolition squad returned and with the help of the police destroyed the huts and took away all the building materials.

Ten months later the residents made an agreement with the police who said they would leave all the temporary huts in peace. They did come back however and destroyed any huts which had concrete block walls. Three years later Mohammed Nagar is home to 140 families. Most families have moved in from local housing areas to escape paying rent since many of them are unskilled labourers on very low incomes.

Figure 3.14 Case Study: Mohammed Nagar, Karachi

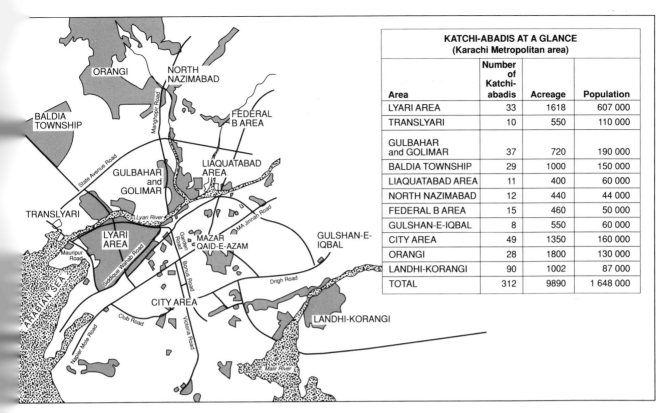

Figure 3.15 *Katchi-abadis* in Karachi

KATCHI-ABADIS AT A GLANCE (Karachi Metropolitan area)			
Area	Number of Katchi-abadis	Acreage	Population
LYARI AREA	33	1618	607 000
TRANSLYARI	10	550	110 000
GULBAHAR and GOLIMAR	37	720	190 000
BALDIA TOWNSHIP	29	1000	150 000
LIAQUATABAD AREA	11	400	60 000
NORTH NAZIMABAD	12	440	44 000
FEDERAL B AREA	15	460	50 000
GULSHAN-E-IQBAL	8	550	60 000
CITY AREA	49	1350	160 000
ORANGI	28	1800	130 000
LANDHI-KORANGI	90	1002	87 000
TOTAL	312	9890	1 648 000

tructure and there is clear ethnic as well as social grouping. The houses, which are often very similar to the rural village types have been improved over the years, and services have been built up in a 'do-it-yourself' fashion with the help of the *dallal* and local business people.

LYARI: Typical Older Katchi-Abadi

Lyari is one of these older settlements situated in the delta of the Lyari River. It has 600 000 inhabitants and is one of the largest popular settlements. The area is becoming more and more densely packed as newcomers arrive. There is no planning at all in the area but it is ideal for jobs as it is so close to the City centre, the SITE (a huge industrial estate) and the Port of Karachi. Because of its ideal location it is sought after by industrialists and speculators. They demolish shanty houses and build four or five-storey tenements with a workshop or shop on the ground floor. Attempts have been made to clear the whole area by demolition but these have been met with local resistance. Some of the plots are used to keep cattle or for storage. Most of the houses are made from cement blocks but the quality is very poor and they are badly affected during rain or floods. Most of the labourers who live in the area (80 per cent) have to walk to work. Services in the area are limited but after a lot of pressure the municipal authorities have put in some water standpoints, garbage dumps and public latrines. Construction and maintenance of these is very poor and because

they cannot cope with the huge numbers involved they are extremely unhealthy. Around the public standpoints there are pools of stagnant water and mud. Garbage is not collected regularly and is left around in piles. One of the latrines had to be demolished because the smell was more than the local residents could stand.

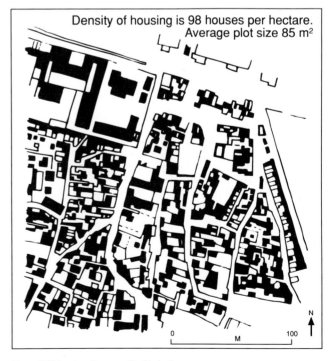

Figure 3.16 Lyari: a city centre *Katchi-abadi*

Density of housing is 98 houses per hectare. Average plot size 85 m²

37

3 Organised Invasions

In some areas, due to the increase in land prices, people cannot afford to use the *dallal* system to acquire a house plot. As a result, some groups have resorted to what have become known as Organised Invasions. They earmark a suitable site, occupy it in the evening and build houses on it during the night, then bribe the authorities to prevent demolition and apply for the legal right to stay. Only a few such invasions have occurred in Karachi so far, but it seems likely that more will occur in future due to the severe lack of available land in convenient locations at prices people can afford.

In the longer-established *katchi-abadis*, especially those where community action has improved conditions, most of the houses are built from bricks or blocks, with proper roofs, and have a reasonable level of facilities such as water, sewerage, garbage collection, storm drainage and electricity. Shanty dwellers are more likely to be given legal rights to their homes if they have been able to provide themselves with basic services. In the early stages of growth the shanty dwellers stand a good chance of being evicted. It is often this threat to their security which encourages inhabitants to join together to resist eviction and demand the improvement of services.

HOUSE TYPES IN A KATCHI-ABADI

Most residents of squatter settlements finance the building of a house from what savings they have, although some are forced to borrow money from friends or money lenders. In some cases the *thallas* (makers of bricks and blocks), on whom the community depends for building materials, will supply them on credit. This is widespread in the *katchi-abadis* in Karachi.

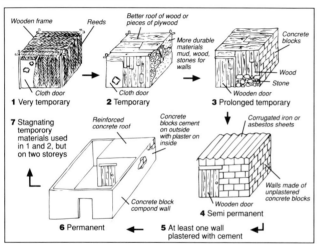

Figure 3.17 House types in a *katchi-abadi*

Most houses begin as a compound wall, one room and a toilet and this is added to over the years so that after ten years the house may have four or five rooms and it may be more than one-storey high. Although masons and other tradespeople are employed, standards are usually poor and the buildings suffer from defects in structure, poor ventilation and similar problems.

Sewerage is the biggest problen and often the most neglected service. In Karachi the systems drain into the *nullas* (natural gullies), where the effluent gathers and slowly soaks away. The health hazards from these practices are serious, particularly where the groundwater is contaminated.

Health care in *katchi abadis* is almost exclusively provided in private clinics, which are usually run by unqualified staff using patent medicines or out-dated drugs to treat patients.

Most children are educated in privately-run schools, run on a purely commercial basis, and geared to how much the residents can afford. They are therefore poorly-built, inadequately ventilated and lit, with poor furniture and resources, and staff are almost all untrained, many of them semi-voluntary.

5 Why is it so difficult for City authorities to stop the growth of *katchi-abadis*?

6 Describe the role of the *dallal* in the creation of *katchi-abadis* in Karachi.

7 Describe the major difference between the planning systems in a British city and Karachi.

8 The City authorities built the new township of North Karachi to try to relieve the pressure on the *katchi-abadis* in the centre of the City. Why was it necessary and why do you think it failed?

9 In what ways has the growth of population in Karachi been caused by political factors outside the control of the City authorities?

SERVICES IN THE KATCHI-ABADI

The development of services in the *katchi-abadis* requires some further explanation, since for the most part not only are the houses illegally built on illegally acquired land, but the services are not provided by the authorities and have to be constructed and developed by the residents themselves.

Water

the early stages of development, water is supplied by wzers (large tankers), usually from the Karachi tropolitan Corporation (KMC) via dallals. Payments arranged through the dallal, who pockets a profit from deal. As the settlement grows, however, these functions are reasingly carried out by local entrepreneurs, who use nkey carts to deliver water from stand pipes directly to tomers.

Electricity

ectricity is provided to those residents who can afford it, ually from diesel generators which are installed and erated by local entrepreneurs. The service is only offered for few homes each evening and on hot afternoons, when air nditioning is required!

Transport

eople also begin to make their own arrangements for ansport; this includes using small Suzuki motor-cycles to rry passengers to and from work and to and from local bus- ops. The operators have no licence or permits, but have come an 'understanding' with the local authority representatives.

Sewerage

n many areas, it is through the efforts of the people emselves that improvements are made, especially when it omes to the installation of sewage systems. Initially simple ools are used to run small pipelines to the nearest nulla or to river bed. However these efforts are often wasted since the ipes are not constructed well enough to stand up to the use nade of them, are not part of an overall planned system and hey quickly block up or fall into disrepair. Since there is an bvious health problem, this is a key area for organised action o take place. The following example illustrates one way out of these difficulties for katchi-abadi dwellers.

ORANGI PILOT PROJECT

In the north western part of Karachi there is a large unauthorised settlement called Orangi, or Orangitown. It contains 750 000 people, and has few basic services. In 1980, a self-help programme called the Orangi Pilot Project (OPP) began with official support to try to help the communities in this settlement area to develop and improve basic services, particularly sanitation.

The Low Cost Sanitation Programme of the OPP is its most successful effort. Through it the OPP has motivated the residents to manage, finance, operate and maintain an underground sewerage system. The OPP designed the system, worked out its costs, and provided tools and supervision while the residents organised themselves, collected the required funds and managed the implementation of the project. Technical research and modification of engineering standards, along with the elimination of contractors' profiteering and kickbacks to officials, have lowered costs to one-quarter of the Karachi Metropolitan Corporation (KMC) rates for similar work. As the people have funded the work they also maintain it. Most of this maintenance is ad-hoc in nature and is a response to a crisis, such as the blockage of a drain resulting in the flooding of a neighbourhood. In some cases people have developed proper neighbourhood organisations that take care of maintenance and charge the residents a regular fee for it. However the OPP system eventually flows into the open nullas, the development of which is beyond the financial and organisational capacity of local people. The OPP has so far assisted the people in providing underground sanitation to about 60 000 housing units.

Further extensions of all these services will depend very much on the efforts of the dallals, who can often succeed in getting political support (in exchange for promised votes, for example) for improved water supplies and proper electrical connections.

EMPLOYMENT IN THE KATCHI-ABADIS

The residents of these settlements have chosen to live there in order to be near the only available types of employment open to them, which is why most come to the City in the first place. In Karachi many of the squatter settlement residents are employed in the chemical and textile industries and are a cheap source of labour. Many have little knowledge of their legal rights in terms of conditions and wages, and may work in dangerous surroundings.

Many women gain work in the garment industry, both in cramped factories and at home (doing piece-work). Similarly, shoe-making is carried on in many katchi-abadis, but it is non-mechanised, with little opportunity for profitable expansion.

Families may also keep buffaloes and cows (see front cover photo), selling the milk produced. Some of the women also make fibre mats, ropes and brooms, with raw materials supplied by an intermediary, who takes most of the profit. There is a thriving business in the recycling of garbage, with glass, plastics, metals and other materials being collected mostly by children, who pass them on to more intermediaries for distribution to manufacturers.

10 In what ways is service provision in the *katchi-abadis* never likely to keep up with population growth?

11 Describe the different ways a *katchi-abadi* dweller might improve an original reed hut.

12 Why are there serious health problems in a *katchi-abadi*?

13 Describe the ways in which services are improved in a *katchi-abadi*.

14 Describe what the residents have to do to get any services in their *katchi-abadi*.

15 What are the advantages and disadvantages of the self-help schemes in the *katchi-abadi*?

16 Describe how the assisted self-help scheme has improved services in Orangi.

17 Describe how the Orangi scheme operates and how it offers a cheaper and more effective method than that normally offered by municipal authorities.

THE OTHER SIDE OF THE STREET

So far, this case study has concentrated on the problems of the *katchi-abadis of* Karachi, in particular the Mohammed Nagar area of Orangi township in the north west part of the City. However, Karachi also contains a number of areas of middle-class and high-income accommodation, many of these dating back to the period of colonial or military domination in the days before Partition.

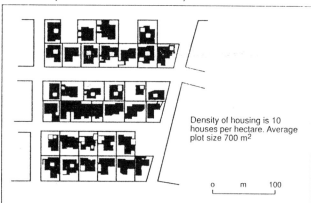

Density of housing is 10 houses per hectare. Average plot size 700 m²

0   m   100

Figure 3.18 Defence society housing in Karachi

	Defence Society	Mohammed Nagar (Orangi Township)
Total area under study (ha)	6.5	4.4
Number of Plots	67.0	230.0
Number of houses	67.0	300.0 +
Density (houses per ha)	10.0	62.0
Public area (ha)	2.0	1.3
Private area (ha)	4.5	3.1
Average plot area (m²)	700.0	135.0
Average built-up area/plot (m²)	285.0	115.0
Average garden area/plot (m²)	415.0	91.0

Figure 3.19 Urban areas data

Figure 3.18 shows the street plan of one such area. The Defence Officers Co-operative Housing Society was set up in 1952 as an independent organisation with the aim of housing military personnel during the chaotic years immediately after the Partition of India and Pakistan. The Society has the legal right to completely control the organisation and planning of the urban landscape in the area under its jurisdiction.

Land was originally purchased at a favourable price from one of the Cantonment Boards which own large areas in and around Karachi. After the housing development was established, with officers being allocated plots by ballot, the management of the area was handed back to the Cantonment Board. Figure 3.19 highlights the contrast between this area and *katchi-abadis* such as Mohammed Nagar.

UPPER-CLASS HOUSING

The houses in this area are large and some are very luxurious; most are designed by architects, have mains water, electricity, gas and drainage systems, and feature large, well-watered gardens and double garages. Only 30 per cent of the owners are actually army personnel, since many of the original owners who acquired plots or houses either sold them at a profit or have leased them out when posted elsewhere.

URBAN DIFFERENCES

There could hardly be a more marked contrast within the boundaries of one city. There are obvious differences in the types and lay-out of the houses. There are also differences in the use of the streets. Newer *katchi-abadis* tend to have a wider planned street lay-out than the older *katchi-abadis* nearer the

itre of town. In Mohammed Nagar however, the
eets themselves are not often used; this is because
-one owns a car, whereas the norm in the Defence
using Society is for two cars per family, and a
sy four-lane road connects this area to the City
ntre.

Water in Mohammed Nagar is provided by 13
ind pipes, which the inhabitants had to pay for
id install themselves, after waiting five years for
rmission to do so from the authorities. In the
efence Society water is piped into every house,
id daily water consumption there amounts to

Figure 3.20 Upper-class housing in Karachi

30 million litres per day – 10 per cent of the total for
the City (the population is about 0.5 per cent of the
City total).

There are no medical or educational facilities at
all in the Mohammed Nagar area, and very few
throughout the whole of Orangi Township. The
cost of travel to other areas is prohibitive, so few
children go to school, and most people are forced to
receive medical help from illegal practitioners.

MUNICIPAL PLANNING

Any improvement in the housing situation in
Karachi is likely to be achieved by co-operation
between the municipal government and the
residents themselves. The Pakistan Government in
the 1960s and 1970s did not have a clear housing
policy and did not plan housing programmes with a
set amount of finance. During this time there were
some special projects. Slums were cleared and low-
cost flats built. But even these were beyond the
financial reach of the poorer sections of society.

Many, like those in North Karachi, were built too
far away from jobs, and families which had been
resettled moved back to the City centre *katchi-abadis*
within a couple of years. Such projects were not
particularly well planned and the low income

groups could only afford them if they were
subsidised. This in turn used up a large amount of
the budget and did not provide enough return to
finance future projects. There was no way this sort
of planning could continue in the long term as all it
did was further drain a limited budget.

KARACHI 2000

The KDA did not have the expertise to produce a
development plan for land use in Karachi. Help was
sought from the United Nations Development
Programme and the World Bank. The UNDP
provided six experts and a joint American-Czech
Planning firm was contracted to execute the
planning work. They came up with three basic
housing development programmes which were
recommended for the lower income groups in the
katchi-abadis.

Improvement and Regularisation Programme (IRP)

This plan was for the lowest income groups.
* *Survey of all unauthorised* katchi-abadis *to see if they could be improved.*
* *Secure land tenure. Most of the* katchi-abadis *were built on land belonging to one of the municipal authorities. If the improvements could be carried out the land ownership could be transferred to the residents. This would give them security so that they could further improve their homes without fear of eviction.*
* *Improvement of public utilities to a basic standard.*
* *Development of a financial plan to achieve the first three aims.*

Open Plot Development (OPD)

This scheme would provide the following.
* *72 m^2 plots.*
* *Secure land tenure.*
* *Public utilities.*
* *Community facilities (schools health centres).*
* *Workshops.*
* *Market place.*

It would provide the initial plans and street lay-outs
in an open space and then the new residents would
have to build their own houses within the planned
area.

Utility Wall Development (UWD)

This is a scheme which has been tried with some
success in countries like Bolivia and Brazil and is
directed towards middle-income groups. Basically in
each plot of land the municipal authorities would
provide a concrete plinth and a concrete core wall as

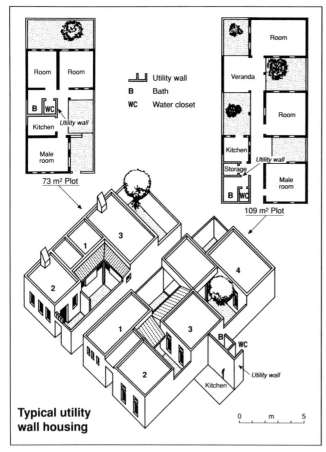

Figure 3.21 Utility wall scheme

21 Why is the OPD plan a good idea for *katchi-abadi* residents on a low income?

22 Referring to figure 3.22, describe the pattern of growth and try to account for the location of the various zones.

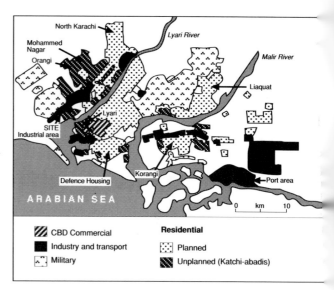

Figure 3.22 Land use map of Karachi

well as water supply and proper drainage. The new residents would have to fit toilet, bath and kitchen facilities and then add on rooms as and when they could afford them. This was a very flexible scheme and offered.the way forward for many thousands of families. This can be seen in figure 3.21.

Unfortunately however good the plan seemed it was extremely restricted by the lack of finance and only a few of these UWD schemes actually succeeded.

18 What are the major differences between housing and services in the middle-class areas and in a *katchi-abadi*?

19 For Karachi briefly describe the planning methods which have been used to try to solve the urban problems.

20 Why is transferring land ownership to a *katchi-abadi* resident seen as a first step to housing improvement?

SUMMARY

- KARACHI'S POPULATION ROSE VERY RAPIDLY AFTER PAKISTAN GAINED INDEPENDENCE BECAUSE OF ITS IMPORTANCE AS A PORT AND INDUSTRIAL CENTRE.
- THE PERCENTAGE OF URBAN DWELLERS IS RISING RAPIDLY LEADING TO SEVERE MANAGEMENT PROBLEMS IN THE PROVISION OF BASIC SERVICES.
- PLANNERS IN KARACHI ARE TRYING TO WORK WITH RESIDENTS OF THE SHANTY TOWNS (*KATCHI-ABADIS*) TO IMPROVE THE PROVISION OF PUBLIC UTILITIES.
- THERE IS NO UNIFIED PLANNING SYSTEM IN KARACHI WITH MANY SHANTY RESIDENTS HAVING TO TRY TO PROVIDE SERVICES FOR THEMSELVES.
- SELF-HELP SCHEMES OFFER THE ONLY HOPE OF IMPROVEMENT IN HOUSING CONDITIONS FOR THE VAST MAJORITY OF SHANTY DWELLERS.

4 URBAN GROWTH: PROBLEMS AND SOLUTIONS

he problems of cities in both MEDCs and LEDCs ave been tackled, until recently, with varying egrees of success largely by the creation and peration of large-scale strategic plans often called master plans'. In many instances these plans were l-conceived, grandiose, and unlikely to succeed for olitical or financial reasons. This type of approach s still used in many parts of the world to attempt to rganise the urban planning process, despite the veaknesses listed below.

THE WEAKNESSES OF STRATEGIC OR MASTER PLANNING

- *Too much time and effort is spent on the preparation of the planning document itself, rather than in achieving any results on the ground.*
- *Most plans are too ambitious, attempting to cover every detail, rather than focusing on key issues.*
- *Plans tend to concentrate on land issues to the detriment of social, economic and environmental issues.*
- *Master plans often reflect a negative view of urban growth, leading to an objective of limiting such growth, regardless of whether or not this is appropriate or even achievable!*
- *Master plans often make unrealistic projections of urban population growth in support of the proposed strategies.*
- *Projections of public investment requirements also tend to be unrealistic.*
- *The separation of the plan-making process is often an inherent weakness (e.g. Karachi: the Karachi Development Authority draws up the five-year plan for housing, but then has to rely on the Karachi Metropolitan Corporation for its implementation).*
- *Detailed rigid zoning plans rarely incorporate the flexibility to react to the economic, social and political forces which really shape the growth of the city.*

In Britain, the response to these problems was to scrap the Development Plan concept first established by the 1947 Town & Country Planning Act, and to replace it with a system of Structure Plans, a process which began in 1968. These plans were intended to provide a broader, strategic framework for subsequent local plans, and to take account of the needs of regional transport, housing and environmental issues. Responsibility for the latter was held by the regions, while the local plans were to be designed and implemented by the districts. The result was that the whole process took a very long time. Where large-scale computer simulations were used in the creation of the structure plans there were conflicts of interest between the two tiers of local government and structure planning became more and more marginalised as the immediate needs of the areas concerned had to be met. These pitfalls were mirrored in the few LEDCs (such as Malaysia) which adopted the particularly British model of structure planning.

In some LEDCs, however, the complete failure of master plans to achieve results led to a pragmatic approach, and a trend towards Action Planning has emerged. Under this approach key urban problems are identified and then the appropriate actions and interventions are carried out subject to the capacity of the authority concerned to undertake them. This is based on a recognition of the urgency of the tasks involved and has been used to ease critical needs for water, sanitation and transportation in several LEDC cities such as Manila and Calcutta (see Figure 4.1).

FUTURE TRENDS IN MANAGING CITIES

The differences between MEDCs and LEDCs in terms of the ways in which urban planning is managed, are often more assumed than real, and in fact recent trends indicate that there are more similarities of approach being adopted year by year. In particular, if there is a common characteristic in these new approaches to urban management, it is probably an increasing realism or pragmatism of approach. This realism is manifested in a number of ways.

- *Realism about urban population growth, accepting that it is neither possible, nor in most cases desirable, to prevent cities from growing. Urban population growth is inevitable and must be planned for and accommodated.*
- *Acknowledgement that the form of cities is determined largely by the desires of individuals or organisations, rather than by governments, and that the private sector will continue to play a dominant role in city development in most parts of the world.*
- *Recognition of the limited ability of governments to intervene in the urban system. A more realistic approach would be one which distinguishes those concerns where government intervention is both essential and can be effected efficiently, from those aspects which are best left to the individual and market forces.*
- *Realism about how much people (especially the poor) can afford to pay for improved urban services and shelter. This applies both to MEDCs and LEDCs.*
- *Recognition that the planning progress cannot be viewed as a tidy, linear sequence of survey–plan–action; rather these stages need to be pursued concurrently and interactively.*
- *Plans need to be flexible and incremental rather than rigid and fixed.*

Another major trend in urban management is the growing recognition of the importance of technological innovations in construction, transportation and communications. The horse-drawn trams of the late nineteenth century made the first commuter suburbs possible. Underground electricity railways allowed the development of denser urban districts. The elevator led to the Manhattan-style central business district, and the telephone, fax, modem and other electronic advances have facilitated the movement to the suburbs of many central business functions, and have encouraged the growth of edge cities in the USA (see figure 5.11, page 47).

Advances in industrial technology have also proved to be critical. The introduction of the conveyer belt and assembly line production made manufacturing in densely developed central city areas less economical and promoted the peripheral industrial estate. Technology advances have facilitated greater mobility for urban residents. This mobility takes three forms.

- **Employment mobility.** *The possibility of changing residence is greater in the city because there are more jobs of greater variety.*
- **Residential mobility.** *In the USA about half of the population changes residence every five years. Residential mobility can be the result of involuntary displacement.*
- **Trip mobility.** *The need to take more and longer local trips is greater in urban areas because of the complex division of functions and greater employment and residential mobility.*

It is ironic that this mobility, an achievement of the modern metropolis, is now in conflict with one of the chief problems of urban planning today – the need to re-establish a closer integration between workplace and residence, not necessarily by placing them under the same roof, but by planning mass transit systems, providing greater flexibility in housing choice and decentralising economic activities throughout the metropolis. Cities will continue to change in the coming decades.

The dynamic growth of the larger cities in the world continues unabated. The city shows no sign of dwindling in size or importance because it does not depend on a single industry or economic activity. The city is no longer a manufacturing town but, rather now reflects a new and complex integration of economic activity, including industry, commerce and services throughout society.

Despite attempts to halt or reverse metropolitan growth, and despite predictions of a return to rural life, the historic trend towards urbanisation is a steady one. One possible manifestation of the present urban metamorphosis is 'spread city' – a city where the central core becomes an entertainment playground for tourists and traditional CBD functions move out to the periphery or edge of the city; more and more work is done from home. This is merely one possible manifestation of the present urban metamorphosis.

> *'Cities are here to stay and we must do the best we can with them.'*
>
> Lauchlin Currie, *Taming the Megalopolis*

1 **Why have Strategic Regional Plans or Master Plans become less common as a tool of urban managers?**

2 **The following five predictions appeared in *The Guardian* in September 1995.**

- **Office-style information labour will continue to increase in proportion to other sorts of work.**
- **Fibre optic cables carrying messages between touch-sensitive terminals will soon make telephone conversations appear to be as crudely mannered as telegrams.**
- **Oil prices will eventually go up drastically in real terms.**
- **The price of computers and telecommunications will keep on falling.**
- **The fashion among employers for contracting work out will become the habit.**

How would these trends affect the growth and development of urban areas?

44

5 ASSIGNMENTS

Doughnut London: Three Decades That Saw City Explode

Refer to Figures 5.1–5.9 and the text in Chapter 2.

1. Between 1961 and 1991 London lost one-third of its population. Give reasons for this decline.

2. Comment on the differences in density between inner and outer London boroughs.

3. Why did so many of the inhabitants of central London, move to elsewhere in the South East?

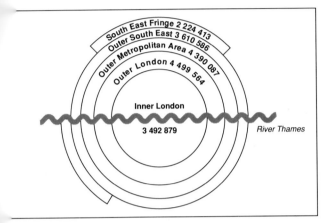

Figure 5.1 1961: Greater London

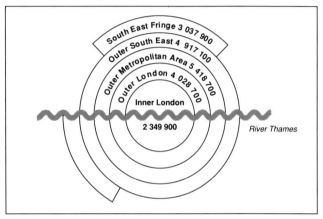

Figure 5.2 1991: 100 mile London

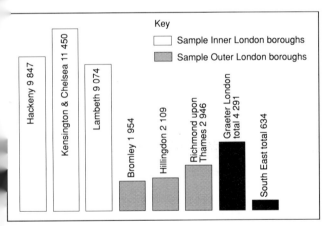

Figure 5.3 A roof over how many heads?

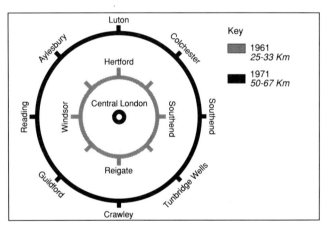

Figure 5.4 Waterloo sunset: commuting old style

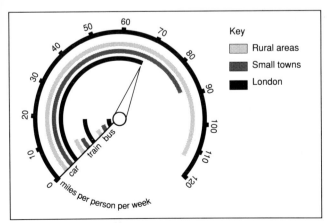

Figure 5.5 The car triumphant

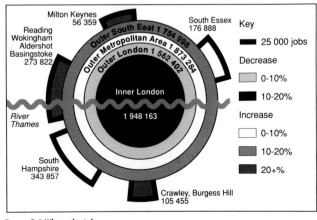

Figure 5.6 Where the jobs went

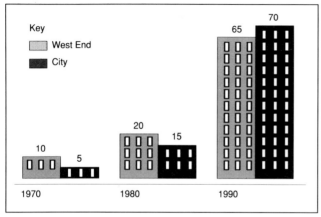

Figure 5.7 Priced out of town

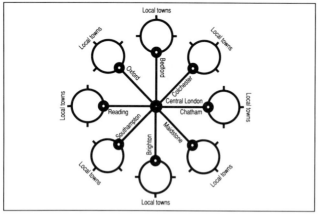

Figure 5.8 The new London

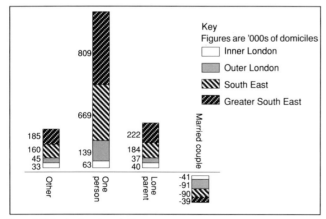

Figure 5.9 The shrinking household

4 **The average speed on London's roads has now fallen to 27.4 kmph peak times, and 31.9 kmph off-peak. In central areas this figure falls even further to 17.4 kmph, irrespective of the time of day. What could be done to ease congestion on London's roads?**

5 **What are the benefits for companies relocating outside London?**

6 **Why has the pressure on housing remained critical, despite the fact that fewer people now live in central London?**

7 **Using Figure 5.12 on the inside cover and an atlas, draw a more detailed model of the 'new London' and its regional network of subcentres.**

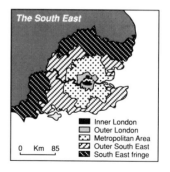

Figure 5.10 The South East

A rapid shift in population has made the old definitions of London redundant. The defunct Greater London Council was a belated attempt in the 1960s to catch up with the fact that the city had spilled far beyond the boundaries of what is called inner London. But even then, the focus of the capital was already shifting further and further towards its edges, into the nebulously defined metropolitan area and beyond.

Blueprint Magazine, February 1992

2 Edge Cities: USA

Edge cities are the latest urban phenomenon identified in the United States. They have been best described by Joel Garreau in his recent book entitled *Edge City – Life on the New Frontier*. Edge cities have been identified as satellite growth points around several of the largest cities in the US. They are mostly located next to intersections on the freeway system. Garreau describes these edge cities as the third wave of urban development in the US. The initial development of the cities was linked with a distinct high-rise and densely packed commercial downtown area. After the 1939–45 war there was an outward movement to the suburbs. This was mainly a residential development and commuters were still linked or shackled to the downtown area for shopping and for jobs. In the 1960s and 1970s developers created large out-of-town shopping malls to serve the huge suburban market. This is the pattern which is being repeated in Britain with many large cities sprouting large out-of-town shopping complexes with countless more planning applications being sought. Garreau and others have identified more than 200 new edge cities in the USA. Jobs have been created as well as houses built.

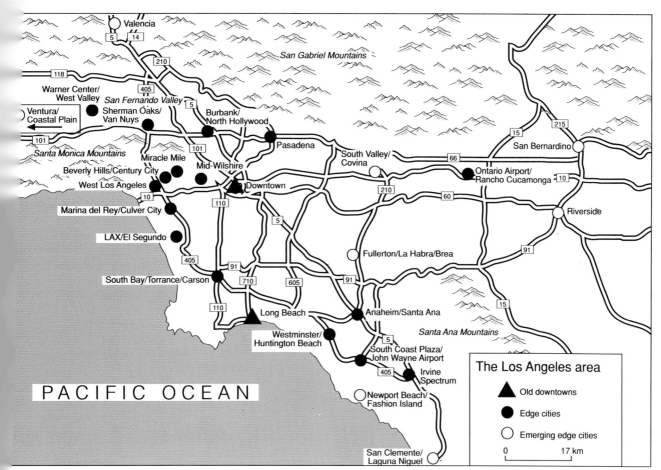

Figure 5.11 Edge cities

These growth points, many of which have no distinct boundary or even a name, now mirror the downtown functions with corporate headquarters, hotels, factories, shops and entertainment etc. The major difference is that there is a much lower residential density and a less intensive commercial agglomeration. There is more space for car parks, and trees and landscaped office blocks are built in open areas. Two-thirds of all office facilities are in edge cities and 80 per cent of these have been built in the last two decades. The pace of this growth can be seen in New York. In the mid-1980s there was more office space in edge cities around New Jersey alone than there was in the downtown area of New York in Manhattan. Some commentators felt that this movement outwards to the edge cities would lead to the demise of the downtown areas. Downtown areas in several cities have, however, gained positive benefits through a reduction in land prices and competition for land. Civic authorities have been able to improve the amenity of their downtown areas and more libraries, parks and theatres have been created. The reduction in the traffic congestion in the city centres has also served to increase the number of visitors because it is now seen as being less of a hassle to visit the downtown areas. Therefore shops have not suffered as much as they had at first feared.

ANATOMY OF AN EDGE CITY

An edge city:
- *has more than 1.5 million m² of leasable office space;*
- *has more than 180 000 m² of leasable retail space;*
- *has more jobs than bedrooms;*
- *is perceived by the general public as one place;*
- *has experienced most growth in the last 30 years.*

8 **Why has the development of edge cities helped old downtown areas and not led to their demise?**

9 **Referring to figure 5.11 make a list of the edge cities found at intersections of the freeway.**

10 **Draw a map of the edge cities around Los Angeles. Refer to Figure 5.12 on the inside cover.**

11 **If there were no planning restrictions where would the edge cities develop around the M25? Give your reasons.**

12 **Refer to figure 5.12 and identify any towns which might already be described as edge cities.**

13 **Describe how you would go about doing the research to prove that a particular place exemplified the main features of an edge city.**

Bibliography

Chapter 1

Systematic Geography, B Knapp, Allen and Unwin, 1988.
Urban geography: Models and Concepts, Gordon and Dick, Holmes McDougall, 1980.
The Changing Towns and Cities, A J Morton, Schofield and Sims, 1988.
Geography: An Integrated Approach, D Waugh, Nelson, 1990.
Urbanisation in the Third World, Potter, Oxford University Press, 1992.
Human Geography: Concepts and Applications, K Briggs, Hodder and Stoughton, 1982.
World Contrasts, B Nixon, Bell and Hyman, 1986.
World Wide Issues in Human Geography, C Hart, Collins, 1987.
The Third World, Beddis, Oxford University Press, 1988.
Elements of Human Geography, Whynne-Hammond, Allen and Unwin, 1987.
Unesco Statistical Handbook, 1991.
The Progress of World Urbanisation, Mountjoy, *Geography*, Volume 71, 1986.
Counterurbanisation – A Rural Perspective, Cooke, *Geography*, Volume 70, 1985.

Chapter 2

Metropolis Now: London and its Region, J M Hall, Cambridge University Press, 1990.
Planning Processes: An introduction for Geographers, J Herington, Cambridge University Press, 1989.
London in the 1990s, B Lenon, Geographical Association, 1993.
Urban Process and Power, P Ambrose, Routledge, 1994.
London: Problems of Change, ed H Clout and P Wood, Longman, 1986.
A New London, R Rogers, M Fisher, Penguin, 1992.
Cities and Services, S Pinch, Routledge, 1985.
The Elusive City, J Barnett, Herbert Press, 1986.
County of London Plan 1943, P Abercrombie, Macmillan, 1943.
Cities in Transition, M Middleton, Michael Joseph, 1991.
London Docklands, ed P Ogden, Cambridge University Press, 1992.
London: A new Metropolitan Geography, ed K Haggart, D Green, Edward Arnold, 1991.
Urban and Regional Planning, P Hall, Routledge, 1992.
London 2001, P Hall, Unwin Hyman, 1989.
Planning London, ed James Simmie, UCL Press, 1994.
Urban Growth and Change in Britain, P Lawless, F Brown, Paul Chapman Publishers, 1986.
Britain in Today's World, Knapp, Unwin Hyman, 1988.
London, B Lenon, Unwin Hyman, 1988.

Chapter 3

A Concise History of Indo-Pakistan, Mahmud, Oxford University Press, 1988.
Between Basti dwellers and Beaurocrats, ed Van der Linden, Pergamon, 1988.
Squatter Citizen, Hardoy, Satterthwaite, Earthscan, 1989.
Karachi: The Show Window of Sind, Hanif Raza, Editions Mystique, Karachi, 1985.
Spectrum guide to Pakistan, Camerapix, 1989.
Planning and development in Pakistan, Quershi, Vanguard, 1984.
Karachi Development Plan 2000, Karachi Devolopment Authority, 1990.
Karachi Master Plan 2000 Report, Karachi Development Authority, 1989.
Development and Health in Pakistan, A Doherty, Commonwealth Institute, 1992.
North–South Programme For Survival, Brandt Commission, Pan, 1980.
The New Landscape – Urbanisation in the Third World, C Correa, Mimar Books, 1989.
Profiles of Five Pakistani Cities, Hasan, 1990.
The Third World City, D D Smith, Methuen, 1987.
Urban Planning Practice in Developing World Countries, Taylor, Williams, Pergamon, 1982.
The Dynamics of Changing Ethnic Boundaries, Case Study of Karachi, Pakistan Development Review, 1990.
London Facts and Figures; 1995 edition, HMSO 1995.
The Times London History Atlas, edited by Hugh Clout, Times Books, 1991.

Chapter 4

Regenerating the Inner City, ed D Donnison, A Middleton, Routledge Kegan Paul, 1987.
Land Use, A S Mather, Longman, 1986.
History of Urban Form, A E J Morris, Longman Scientific, 1994.
Metropolis 2000 Planning Poverty and Politics, T Angotti, Routledge, 1993.
Managing Fast Growing Cities, ed Nick Devas & Carole Rakodi, Longman Scientific & Technical, 1993.
Cities are Good for Us, Harley Sherlock, Paladin, 1991.

Chapter 5

Doughnut London, Blueprint Magazine, February 1992.
Edge City, Joel Garreau, Doubleday, 1991.